Mary Bell
The Real Story

Luke Armitage

Contents

SLIDING DOORS

Mary Flora Bell was born in Corbridge in 1957. Corbridge is a village in Northumberland, sixteen miles west of Newcastle. The village was one of the most northern points of the Roman Empire and where the future Manchester United captain Steve Bruce was born. It was in the suburb of Scotswood, in a South West district of Newcastle though that Mary Bell's infamous crimes would take place. Mary Bell's Scotswood was a place of puddles and concrete but there were open spaces within walking distance of the bleak little houses where she and her family and neighbours lived.

The broad strokes of the Mary Bell story are familiar to anyone with an interest in true crime but the specifics are not quite as clear cut in places as is sometimes made out. A common theme in many accounts of this case is that Mary Bell was an unusually intelligent and shrewd little girl who ran rings around everyone. The truth is that Mary displayed little academic or criminal intelligence but plenty of predictable childlike naivety once the law caught up with her. She really wasn't that smart. Mary Bell was a confident and gobby child but these qualities were of no value to her in police custody and a court of law. Mary Bell was not Rhoda Penmark in The Bad Seed or Damien Thorn in The Omen. She wasn't a supernatural horror villain but simply a disturbed girl of average intelligence.

Mary Bell's mother was Elizabeth "Betty" Bell (née McCrickett). Betty was born in 1940 in Glasgow and Mary was the second of her four children. Betty (no one called her Elizabeth) was seventeen when she gave birth to Mary Bell. Mary Bell was always called 'May' by her family and friends so mother and daughter shared this little quirk where no one ever called them by their full birth name. Betty Bell married a man named Billy Bell not long after becoming a mother. We do not know if Billy Bell was Mary Bell's biological father (the general consensus seems to be that he probably wasn't) but it didn't really matter because he was the only father she knew. Billy Bell (an unmistakable figure in the local area due to his size and reddish hair) was a drunk who had served time in prison for armed robbery. He was known to be quite a dangerous man. However, though you wouldn't guess from his unpleasant capsule biography, Billy Bell was kind and caring with Mary Bell and one of the few people in her childhood she ever had any genuine affection towards. The only problem is that Billy Bell often spent more time in the pub or in prison than he did at home. This largely relegates him to an enigmatic and frustrating footnote in the Mary Bell story.

Mary Bell had two sisters and a brother. Space was at a premium in the house they lived in on Whitehouse Road. Conditions were spartan by today's standards. The house was cold in the winter and Mary had to sleep in a back room downstairs. Mary Bell would not recognise much of Scotswood today - where new houses can sell for over £200,000. The world Mary Bell grew up in was a grainy kitchen sink pease pudding for tea black and white film just a few decades on from the war. Mary Bell's siblings remain something of a mystery in her story because, as you might have guessed, they have never been very keen to talk about their child murdering sister. Mary Bell was locked up at the age of eleven in 1968 and then released and given a new identity in the early 1980s. Although she did meet her siblings again as an adult she said it was like meeting strangers. They didn't really want much to do with her. This is some sort of explanation for why Mary somehow, for the most part at least, remained close to her mother through her life.

Her mother was all Mary Bell had left for a while - until that is she started to form adult romantic relationships for the first time. Betty Bell was not a mentally stable woman. Most people who encountered her (including the police and her sisters Isa and Catherine) thought she was crazy. Mary Bell was taken to hospital several times for injuries suffered while in the care of her mother. There were overdoses of painkillers and sleeping pills and household accidents. Mary Bell was also dropped from a first floor window by her mother when she was three years old. The sneaking suspicion that Betty Bell was trying to get rid of Mary was confirmed when she took her daughter to an adoption agency and basically sold Mary Bell to a childless woman who was about to emigrate to Australia. The childless woman even bought some dresses for Mary Bell in anticipation of their new life together thousands of miles away.

This was a genuine sliding doors moment. Had this gone ahead, there would have been no 'Tyneside Strangler' or tragic child murders in late sixties Scotswood. There wouldn't even have been a Mary Bell because her name would have been changed. Mary would have grown up on the other side of the world as an Australian. But it was not to be. Mary Bell's Aunt Catherine learned of the transaction and was outraged. Catherine put a stop to the adoption and returned Mary Bell to Whitehouse Road - where she would continue to grow up as a Geordie and definitely not an Australian. Betty's sisters Catherine and Isa offered more than once to have custody of Mary but Betty would not agree to this. It was odd that Betty was willing to give Mary to a complete stranger (who she knew nothing about) but not her own sisters. There was a perverse sense of pride which blocked Betty from doing this. She didn't want her family to think she was incapable of caring for her daughter.

Mary Bell's childhood saw her sustain more than one head injury. A surprisingly high number of killers received head injuries from an accident in their childhood or youth. There is a theory that this impairs the part of the brain responsible for ruminating on the consequences of one's actions. Mary Bell was also a bed wetter - which is also (a lot more questionably) also occasionally held up as some sort of warning sign that someone might be destined for dark things. When she was about five, Mary Bell witnessed one of her friends being hit and killed by a local bus. This incident was not something which she shook off and forgot about - despite her young age. It seemed to activate some sort of latent darkness within Mary Bell and change her personality. Teachers who encountered her at nursery and early schooling noticed that Mary Bell could be mean spirited and unpredictable when it came to other children. She had sudden tantrums and got angry very easily. Mary Bell's mother displayed classic symptoms of being bipolar and Mary seemed to be following in Betty's footsteps.

The most common photograph of Mary Bell online is a blurred black and white picture of her as a small child smiling for the camera with a bob haircut. This misleading photograph is responsible for the perception of Mary Bell as some cute angelic looking child who was secretly evil. In reality, Mary Bell was plain looking and later no beauty as a teenager or adult. Mary Bell's best friend was a scruffy sad-eyed girl named Norma Joyce Bell. The pair were not related but lived in the same street (Mary lived at number 70 while Norma lived at number 68). Norma (born in 1955) was two years older than Mary Bell and much taller. The standard portrayal of Norma in the Mary Bell story is that she was a 'feeble minded' (words actually spoken at the trial) innocent girl who was manipulated and dominated by Mary Bell. The truth is more complicated. Forensic evidence proved that Norma Joyce Bell was present at the second murder scene and Norma admitted this herself. Norma also wrote poetry as a hobby - which contradicted the portrait of her as 'feeble minded' and stupid.

Norma, on the instruction of her family, was also smart enough to understand that in order to avoid serious punishment she needed to quickly terminate any vestige of loyalty or affection she had for Mary Bell. The thing which saved Norma more than anything was the perception that she was only capable of bad things in the company of Mary Bell while Mary Bell was capable of bad things with or without Norma. Norma was largely absolved of any blame by the legal system. Norma Joyce Bell is one of the more inscrutable components of the Mary Bell story. She was Mary Bell's forgotten sidekick. Norma Joyce Bell is generally portrayed as an innocent girl who maybe had some learning difficulties. This made her malleable and easily led. While it is questionable that Norma was quite as innocent and stupid as is sometimes made out, she was still better than Mary Bell. Norma only ever got into trouble when she was in the company of Mary Bell. If she had any sense, Norma would have ditched Mary Bell and saved herself a lot of trouble.

Mary Bell's mother Betty worked as a prostitute. In the telling of the Mary Bell story this has sometimes snowballed into Betty being a notorious and popular local dominatrix who had a fully equipped dungeon in one of the rooms of her house on Whitehouse Road. The reality is that Betty never had much money so it seems very unlikely this was true. Betty actually made Mary's cotton dresses herself to save money. Mary Bell's brother and sisters contested the claim that Betty was some highly sought after local sex worker who had turned her house in a brothel or dungeon. They said they never saw any evidence of that. Not to say that Betty wasn't a prostitute because she was (social workers said Betty even confessed to having a few whips in the house) and she most likely did bring a few 'customers' back to the house from time to time.

Betty also visited Glasgow (where she had relatives) and worked as a prostitute there too. Betty Bell was a tired looking woman who wore a terrible blonde wig and always seemed to look miserable. She wasn't exactly a high class expensive escort. We now have a general picture of Mary Bell's home life. Billy Bell was often in the pub and sometimes in prison. Betty (who had a drinking problem) was a prostitute who spent a lot of time in Glasgow. This is not a nice picture. While she did have some pleasant isolated memories of childhood (Mary Bell said that things were fine when Billy was home), the erratic moods of her mother and a general aura of poverty made life less than idyllic for Mary. Betty Bell was a very strange and troubled woman. She once told one of her sisters that Mary had been run over by a lorry when in reality Mary was fine and just staying at someone else's house. Betty Bell was someone who liked attention and sympathy - even if she had to say and do bizarre things to get that attention and sympathy.

At this point in the Mary Bell story it is claimed that Betty used Mary as a sort of prop in the domination sessions she conducted at home as a prostitute. Mary, so the story goes, was forced from the age of about four or five to have sex with some of the men that Betty brought home. Mary, it is claimed, was whipped and beaten, even strangled, in some of these sessions. The basic claim then is that Betty catered to sado masochistic paedophiles in Newcastle and acted as a pimp for her little daughter. And this, allegedly, all goes a long way to explaining why Mary Bell became Mary Bell. Why she became a killer. The Tyneside Strangler was thus explained. It was all Betty Bell's fault. And what was the source for this shocking revelation? It was Mary Bell herself. Mary only spoke of this alleged sexual abuse in an interview for a book many decades later. Conveniently, she only disclosed this information when Betty Bell was dead and in no position to offer a response.

Mary Bell had two sisters but neither of them experienced any sexual abuse and were unaware of anything like this happening to Mary. Why would Betty single out Mary in this way? Billy Bell was not away all the time either. Billy Bell had his flaws but he loved Mary and he was a formidable man who you wouldn't want to get on the wrong side of. He truly didn't seem the type to stand idly by while Mary was passed around to any local paedophile who happened to be passing Whitehouse Road. Despite the later allegations of sexual abuse, Mary Bell was never estranged from her mother. They even lived together for a period years later when Mary was an adult. Betty Bell could be violent, drunken, unpredictable, and bad tempered, that much is established, but the notion she was the heartless sadistic ringleader of some underground Newcastle paedophile ring which revolved around sexually abusing and hurting her daughter is not as easy to believe.

Norma Joyce Bell attended Whickham View Benwall Lower School - which these days is part of Newcastle College. The art deco school was built in the 1930s. Mary Bell, meanwhile, attended Delaval Road Junior School. Despite this the pair were as thick as thieves thanks to living only two doors away from each other. There is plenty of evidence that Mary and Norma were bullies when it came to the local kids. They were not nice at all. The most disturbing facet of this was Mary's fascination with younger children. Mary found the concept of hurting little kids who were much younger, weaker and smaller than her very alluring. She enjoyed having this sense of power and dominance over another human being. This is, I need hardly remind you, the standard mindset of your average serial killer. There was something broken inside Mary Bell. She wasn't right in the head. In many accounts of the Mary Bell story this is all explained away by the alleged sexual abuse. Mary was allegedly abused and dominated by men and so her crimes were (so the explanation goes) some sort of way to turn the tables and assert her own power.

Mary Bell's first ever conviction for was 'larceny' of a gas meter. Norma was also present during this crime. The detective who arrested Mary Bell was Peter Moore. Mr Moore later said that when he interviewed Mary Bell with her mother, Mary, despite being ten years-old, already had the air of a streetwise criminal and would answer with "no comment" to any tricky question thrown her way. Mary and Norma, in light of their age, were conditionally discharged because this was their first offence. Peter Moore said that after the case Betty Bell sought him out for a private chat and had a go at him for taking two little girls to court. Betty was furious. Peter Moore said he told Betty Bell, once she'd calmed down, that if she didn't supervise her daughter more responsibly in the future then Mary would end up in court again for something a lot more serious than robbing gas meters. The reason why Mary and Norma didn't attract the attention of social services in the way you might expect is that both of them had good school attendance records and both of them had reasonably clean clothes and seemed well fed. On the surface, there were no major problems immediately apparent.

In the late spring of 1968, Mary Bell (still ten years-old) and Norma were questioned by the police when a three year-old boy (who was not named in police documents but was John Best -a distant cousin of Mary) was found crying with blood coming from a wound on his head. The last time anyone had seen the boy before the injury he was with Mary and Norma. The two girls had pushed the boy off a ledge and caused the injury themselves. They had then abandoned the confused and distressed child. Mary and Norma were required to give statements to the police but nothing came of this and the police decided the incident must have been an accident. In their statements to the police Mary and Norma pretended that the boy was already injured (when they saw him for the second time that day) and they had merely offered assistance. This story would have quickly been exposed in any thorough investigation but the police decided that since the boy was now home and fine they had more important things to do with their time.

The same day as the incident with the boy, Mary Bell attacked seven year-old Pauline Watson at a nursery sandpit where children were playing. Norma was present (though at thirteen she was getting long in the tooth to be playing in the nursery with six and seven year-olds) but not involved in the attack. Mary and Norma had got into the nursery through a hole in the fence. The trouble all started when Mary ordered Pauline to get out of the sandpit. Pauline, who was playing in the sandpit with two of her friends, refused to get out of the sandpit and Mary reacted by trying to throttle her and shoving sand in her mouth. Mary then tried to do the same to Pauline's friend Susan Cornish. Pauline said she had never seen Mary Bell before and had no idea who she was. Mary had wanted the sandpit for herself and decided that fear and violence was the best way to achieve that ambition. The mother of Pauline Watson was not happy at all when she heard what had happened and made a complaint to the police. Mary and Norma were therefore required once again to give statements to the local police station.

In her statement, Mary said that she was playing when she heard a scream. When she asked Norma what had happened, Norma said that Pauline Watson had fallen and injured her throat. That was the basis of Mary Bell's statement. Mary cast herself as an innocent party oblivious to all the trouble. Norma's police statement was very different. Norma said that Mary Bell tried to strangle Pauline after Pauline had said she was willing to fight Mary if she had to. Norma said she tried to stop Mary but Mary ignored her. Norma said that Mary then did the same to Pauline's friend Susan Cornish. Pauline Watson had been eating a stick of rock in the nursery and Norma said Mary had taken the rock from Pauline after the incident and then left. Norma's police statement claimed that Pauline Watson had begun to turn purple when Mary was throttling her. Norma said she was frightened by this and knew there would be trouble. The most chilling line of Norma's statement was her recollection of Mary asking Pauline if someone would die if their neck was squeezed.

Norma's police statement ended with the promise that she wasn't friends with Mary Bell anymore (which wasn't true). It was a very shrewd coda by Norma - or whoever might have instructed her to say that. Aside from her claim that she and Mary Bell were now permanently estranged, Norma simply told the truth in her statement. She wasn't scared into silence by her crazy friend. Betty Bell got involved in the sandpit incident and asked the nursery teacher to get to the bottom of the affair. In the end the police decided that because there were no visible injuries on the two alleged victims there wasn't much they could do besides issue Mary and Norma with a warning to stay out of trouble and leave the other children alone. Pauline Watson's mother was told by the police that if she wished she had the right to take out a private summons for an assault on her child but Mrs Watson decided not to do this.

Mary Bell was becoming a terrible bully. Her teacher Eric Foster later said he once had to tell Mary off for stubbing out a cigarette on another girl's cheek. Mr Foster said that Mary admitted doing this and acted as if it was no big deal. Despite the sandpit trouble, Mary and Norma liked one another. They made each other laugh. Other kids used to joke that if Mary told Norma to jump off the Tyne Bridge then Norma would have happily jumped off the Tyne Bridge. It would be stating the obvious to point out that Mary Bell was a bad influence on Norma. Norma would not have got into trouble on her own or with other kids but she was constantly getting into trouble with Mary Bell. Norma had ten siblings so her house was crowded and money was tight. Her family life was, despite this, much more stable and loving than that of Mary Bell. Norma's mother was a decent woman who took her responsibilities as a parent a lot more seriously than Betty Bell.

Norma was asking for trouble by having Mary Bell as her best friend. The adults on Whitehouse Road didn't know that little 'May' at number 70 was a psychopath. Mary was in and out of neighbours' houses and a familiar face on those streets. She was a cheeky and normal kid as far as the adults were concerned. It was only the teachers at school and other children who were witness to the darker side of Mary Bell. One of Mary Bell's teachers later told the newspapers she was a stroppy child who would hit, pinch, and even try to throttle other children. Mary seemed to be incapable of forming friendships with other kids with Norma being the sole exception. Mary Bell and Norma, like many children in Scotswood, would cross the railway tracks to play in an area where a lot of construction work was taking place. In a dirty maze of concrete blocks and bags of cement the children would play hide and seek or just explore out of curiosity. The construction and building sites were a result of slum terraces being torn down to build new houses. A big patch of waste ground in this area was called the Tin Lizzie by local kids and a popular place for them to go and play.

I MURDER SO THAT I MAY COME BACK

There are very few photographs of Mary Bell as a child on the internet. A couple which purport to be Mary are even fakes. This is what gives the photo of a smiling Mary Bell with the bob haircut such power. It became the defining image of Mary - despite the fact that she didn't look much like that in real life. If someone writes an e-book about Mary Bell this is the picture which they inevitably want to use for their cover. This creates a perception that the Mary Bell who murdered two children was that tiny angelic looking girl with the bob haircut. By 1968 though there was something feral and wild about Mary Bell. She had more of a scrappy tomboy haircut and her blue eyes were set wide apart. Her mouth frowned downwards and her upturned nose had a slightly dented quality like a boxer who had been punched in the face a few too many times. Mary wasn't too happy about her life in Scotswood and dreamed of going to live with a grandparent in Scotland. Mary wasn't like other girls. She didn't dream of being a princess or a famous singer. Mary's greatest fantasy was to be a famous criminal. She and Norma would sometimes pretend they were notorious bank robbers or outlaws.

1968 seems like a long time ago today but it certainly wasn't a bygone dark age. The Beatles, The Doors, Marvin Gaye, and Joni Mitchell were making music. Elvis made his triumphant '68 Special television comeback. British fashion was seen as hip and trendsetting. The big films at the cinema that year were 2001: A Space Odyssey, Funny Girl, Planet of the Apes, The Odd Couple, Oliver!, and Rosemary's Baby. On television in 1968, Mary Bell would have watched things like Top of the Pops, Captain Scarlet and the Mysterons, The Avengers, The Prisoner, Blue Peter, Please Sir!, Doctor Who, Jackanory, It's a Knockout, and Animal Magic. There were also popular American imports like Star Trek, Batman, The Monkees, and Bewitched. Television had more power in 1968 than it does today. Aside from radio it had no serious rival. The fuzzy cathode ray tube transported people out of their humdrum lives. The television at number 70 Whitehouse Road was on at all hours. Mary used it as a temporary way to escape from her troubled life at home with the unpredictable Betty Bell.

Norma Joyce Bell was different to Mary in that she had other friends and found it easier to get along with other kids. Norma didn't really need Mary Bell but there was something about Mary which she seemed to be attracted to. Maybe it was that sense of danger and excitement. It would be wrong to presume though that Norma hung around with Mary purely out of morbid curiosity. These two girls had a genuine and unique bond of friendship that only children can have. What didn't help Norma at all was that Mary lived two doors down.

It was impossible for her to avoid Mary Bell because Mary was practically the next door neighbour. So by 1968 these two children spent much of their time in the company of one another. They would go wandering through the streets and ruins of Scotswood, stopping off to buy a bag of sweets, bumping into cousins or siblings along the way. There was by now a terrifying darkness bubbling up inside Mary Bell. Teachers and nursery staff who had encountered Mary Bell over the years had sometimes noticed that Mary was strange in the way she rarely displayed any emotion. She didn't laugh or cry or get happy or sad like other children. Mary Bell was an oddly blank and unemotional child who seemed to live deep within herself.

Mary Bell killed for the first time on Saturday the 25th of May 1968. It was the day before she turned eleven years old. The murder took place at 85 St Margaret's Road in the upstairs bedroom of a derelict house that was due for demolition. The area was unofficially known as Rat Alley due to the dereliction and the fact that local children were drawn there like moths to a flame. Mary Bell was alone when the murder took place. Norma, her inseparable sidekick, was not present. The victim was a four year-old boy named Martin Brown. Martin, unfortunately for him, had been exploring Rat Alley and ended up running into Mary Bell. It seems, from most accounts, that Martin had noticed Mary Bell while out and about and started following her around and tagging along. Martin knew Mary Bell quite well and trusted her. He thought they were friends. It is more than likely that Mary might even have babysat for Martin in the past. This context gives you a good insight into what an evil child Mary Bell truly was.

Mary Bell used her superior strength and size (she was seven years older than Martin) to squeeze Martin's neck until he choked and couldn't breathe. Martin passed out and his life slipped away. When this happened Mary left the scene but she would soon return. She had no instinct to help Martin Brown or find an adult. She just left him to die. The murder is almost unbearable to contemplate because the victim was so young, innocent, and vulnerable. If this happened today, Mary Bell would be as despised and hated as Jon Venables and Robert Thompson. People would wish her serious harm or worse. Not to say that Mary Bell did not elicit hatred and anger in 1968 because she did. Things were just more reserved and less magnified and hysterical in those times before the internet and news channels.

In 1968 there had never been a high profile criminal case in the United Kingdom where someone as young as Mary Bell had committed murder. We have, tragically, had a few since 1968 but not many. It is exceptionally rare for someone as young as ten to commit a murder and rarer still in Britain. This is why the case of Mary Bell still holds a morbid fascination over fifty years on. It is difficult to get your head around a little girl of ten/eleven murdering a younger child not just once but twice. We do not know what Mary Bell would have done next if she hadn't been caught but it doesn't seem unreasonable to fear that she would have killed again. Mary Bell, in basic terms, was shaping up to be the world's youngest serial killer. Mary Bell would later say that she meant the victims no harm and didn't understand the concept of death in 1968. Both of these claims seem highly doubtful at best. Mary Bell's mood after murdering Martin Brown can only be described as one of elation. She was tremendously excited and fascinated by all the drama which followed. There wasn't a shred of remorse. Mary Bell had just shattered the life of Martin Brown's mother but she appeared to take pleasure in this fact.

Martin Brown was found by some children late in the afternoon. There was some blood and the children were scared. Not too far from the house there were some workmen doing a weekend shift. The children ran to the workmen and told them what they had found. One of the workmen, a man named John Hall, tried to perform CPR on Martin Brown. An ambulance was called for and Martin was taken to hospital where doctors confirmed that he had died and couldn't be saved. Before the ambulance arrived a group of children had massed around the derelict house in an attempt to see what was happening. The children included Mary Bell and Norma. Mary Bell had excitedly gone to find Norma and informed her that something had happened in Rat Alley which they should go and investigate. It was all a game to Mary Bell. She was having the time of her life. When the first book about Mary Bell was published in the 1970s the book blamed many things for the way she turned out and the murders she committed. Society was blamed. The social services were blamed. Betty Bell was blamed. The legal system was criticised. What didn't seem to be blamed was Mary Bell. The same Mary Bell who throttled two children to death and then had great fun wallowing in the aftermath of all the misery and sadness she had created.

Another thing, besides the youth of the killer, which makes the Mary Bell case so unusual and unsettling is that the perpetrator was a girl. This is very rare though it has happened in some countries. On June the 1st, 2004, two girls were together in an empty classroom at an elementary school in the city of Sasebo in Nagasaki Prefecture in Japan. One of the girls was Satomi Mitarai - who was twelve years-old. The other girl was never officially named by the Japanese authorities and became known simply as 'Girl A' in this ghastly case (under Japanese law, juvenile offenders are not allowed to have their identity revealed). Girl A was only eleven years-old. A teacher had eventually noticed the two girls were missing and not in their allocated class. Girl A then appeared and calmly sat down down. Her clothes were clearly stained with what looked like blood. When the teacher went to look for the other girl a tragic and horrifying discovery awaited. Satomi Mitarai was dead. Her throat had been slashed. There were also extensive wounds to her arms. Girl A had used a box cutter (known as a Stanley knife in Britain) to viciously murder her friend. Satomi had been left to bleed to death.

Girl A had essentially tricked Satomi Mitarai in the classroom by telling her they were playing a game. She had taken the victim's glasses off and told her to close her eyes. After this she struck with the knife. As a coda to this harrowing attack she had slashed Satomi Mitarai's wrists. Though paramedics were called for it was sadly too late to save the young victim of this awful attack. She was rushed to hospital but died of her injuries. Girl A had apparently said "I did a bad thing" when she sat down again in the classroom. It later transpired that Girl A and Satomi Mitarai were once good friends who played on a basketball team together. However, the girls had eventually fallen out. The main source of friction was the fact that Girl A believed that Satomi Mitarai had posted some mean messages about her on the net. There was apparently some back and forth between them in cyberspace. Both girls were apparently quite tech savvy and had their own blogs and websites. They evidently took these blogs very seriously and Girl A in particular was very thin skinned and sensitive - even for an eleven year-old. She was furious to see that her friend had been critical of her.

Girl A had then lured Satomi Mitarai to the empty classroom and tried to blindfold her. In the end she covered Mitarai's eyes with her hand and stabbed her in the neck. Some weeks before Girl A had apparently threatened a boy in school with a knife - though this incident had clearly gone unreported at the time and nothing was made of it. The knife wound which killed Satomi Mitarai was very deep. In some reports in Japan it was said that the girl was nearly decapitated. A twelve year-old girl is likely to have a very small neck but it was evident too that a frightening amount of force had been used for one so young. Satomi Mitarai dropped to the floor and tried to crawl to the door but tragically her young life was nearly at an end. This incident was naturally one that shocked Japan. Girl A was taken out of society and sentenced to a juvenile correctional facility. The person one felt sorry for the most was Satomi Mitarai's father. He had already lost his wife three years ago and now he'd lost his beloved daughter too.

Much was made of the fact that Girl A loved horror films (she apparently had a website full of horror imagery) and video games. In particular her fondness for Battle Royale was cited as a factor in what she had done. There was certainly a pushback against this hysteria though. Most children play computer games without any harmful consequences. It isn't as if everyone who ever played a video game or watched Battle Royale turned into Girl A. Girl A's real name was Tsuji Natsumi. She had a very high IQ and had seemed like a normal child to those the knew her. The authorities found no evidence that Girl A suffered from mental illness or had any condition which impaired her thinking. In fact they found that she had calmly planned the murder of Satomi Mitarai with a cold and clinical thoroughness which was shocking to consider given her age. They judged that she suffered from Hikikomori Syndrome - which basically means someone who is alienated and wants to isolate themselves from society and enter a state of isolation. That was all very interesting but it wasn't much of an explanation for why she killed her friend with a Stanley knife.

Tsuji Natsumi said she had considered killing her friend with an ice-pick or by strangulation before she settled on using a knife. She had clearly put a lot of thought into this murder. Tsuji Natsumi's father apologised to Satomi Mitarai's family. He was so distraught by what his daughter had done that he took his own life. It was just a very tragic and shocking case - all the more so because the killer was a little girl. In contrast to some other 'killer kids' (like Mary Bell), Girl A did at least have remorse for her crime which seemed genuine. She cried in police custody and said she was sorry for what she had done. Natsumi seemed to immediately regret her actions - which is something you definitely can't say about many other infamous juvenile killers. Most of them would have happily killed again given half a chance but that wasn't the case with Girl A. It was therefore judged that she could be rehabilitated.

In the last school photo taken of Girl A and her victim they are in a group photo and both smiling. Tsuji Natsumi was wearing wearing a blue top with 'Nevada' written on it. This led to her becoming known in the media and online world as Nevada-Tan. Tan means 'little'. The 'character' of Nevada-Tan became something of an icon in some anime and online circles - which was in very questionable taste. There were even tales of how a blood splattered 'Nevada-Tan' had posed for a photo on the school stairs after the murder and this picture was supposedly released onto the net. This photograph was a fake though and that aspect of the tragic 'legend' of Girl A was apparently an urban myth. As for Girl A, she was subject to years of counselling and spent some time in an actual prison. In 2013 she was released under supervision and moved to a secret location with her family. It seems that Girl A was rather like Mary Bell, rehabilitated and able to build a new life as she grew older. Her deeds live on though in the form of 'Nevada Tan' - who continues to lurk on on the fringes of the net and even (much like Mary Bell) inspire the names of bands and songs.

Mary Bell knew the family of Martin Brown reasonably well - which makes her murder of Martin even more chilling and cruel. She knew that Martin's mother was a woman named June and also knew a number of Martin's relatives by name.

After she left Rat Alley with Norma, Mary went to the home of Martin's aunt Rita Finlay and told her that something had happened to Martin. Mary had babysat for Rita's kids in the past. Mary was basically prodding this family with a stick to observe their reactions to the tragedy which had befallen them thanks to her. Some children can be cold and uncaring but Mary Bell was in a league of her own. Martin's mother June Brown, a dignified and brave woman who impressed anyone who came into contact with her after this tragedy, later said in an interview that if she had known at the time that little May Bell from Whitehouse Road had killed Martin she doubted she would have been able to restrain herself. June said she would have ended up in prison herself. If four-year Martin Brown had been your child you most likely would have had the same sentiments.

Home Office pathologist Bernard Knight (who is still alive at the time of writing and was later awarded a CBE) conducted a post-mortem on the body of Martin Brown. Knight could find no obvious cause of death because there was no indication of violence or force on the body. The lack of visible brute force was because Martin had been killed by a ten year-old girl. This possibility never occurred to Bernard Knight and the police at the time. For this they can't really be blamed. The identity of the killer in this murder turned out to be completely unexpected and shockingly bizarre. In the room where the body was found there were several empty pill bottles (which, most logically, had been left there by workmen). The police theory was that Martin Brown may have eaten these headache pills thinking they were sweets and overdosed. Bernard Knight could find no conclusive proof that the poisoning theory was correct and so could not confirm the pill explanation. An open verdict was rendered. Martin Brown's death was, officially, a tragic and unexplained accident. No evidence of foul play had been established. Mary Bell had murdered a child and got away with it.

Norma Joyce Bell had seen Martin Brown a couple of times on that Saturday - the day of the murder. She was not though with Mary Bell in the derelict house. Mary Bell did not outright tell Norma what had happened but she liked to hint at what she had done. Later that day, after the murder, Norma went to Mary's house and together they wrote a series of disturbing and bewildering notes which they planned to leave in the nursery. This was the Woodlands Crescent nursery of the sandpit incident fame. The nursery was only a few minutes walk from Mary's house. The next day, Mary Bell's eleventh birthday, Mary and Norma broke into the nursery by removing loose slates from the roof. Once inside they trashed the place, turning desks over and splashing ink everywhere. In the notes, which were left in the classroom and the base of a telephone, Mary and Norma sign off as 'Fanny and Faggot', which were the names of fictional criminals they sometimes pretended to be.

The notes were designed to be cryptic confession notes confessing to Martin Brown's murder. The notion, which still persists, that Mary Bell was a highly intelligent child was contradicted by the composition of these notes. "I murder so THAT I may come back" - "fuch of we murder watch out Fanny and Faggot" - "we did murder Martain brown Fuckof you Bastard" - "You are miceyy Becurse we murdered Martain Go Brown you Bete Look out THERE are Murders about By FANNYAND and auld Faggot you Srcews". The line "I murder so THAT I may come back" was especially curious. What did it mean? Come back to the nursery? Come back to life? Was using the word 'may' a deliberate clue given that everyone called Mary by that name? A common reading of this line is that Mary is suggesting she must murder to become immortal. This sort of stuff played into the later portrayal of Mary Bell as some supernatural horror villain.

Mary and Norma seemed to have a strange obsession with this nursery. The vandalism was revenge and frustration because they were not welcome at the nursery and too old to be playing there anyway. The confession notes were also strange. You could have written it off as a childish bad taste prank were it not for the fact that one of the girls writing the confessions was actually the killer. Mary seemed to love dragging Norma into her dark little world. She liked to have an audience and someone to show off to. It would have been no fun playing all these sick games on her own. The police were called in after the vandalism at the nursery. They didn't think the confession notes had any relevance to anything. It was, as far as the police were concerned, just a couple of mindless vandals and hooligans who couldn't spell very well. The police did point out to the nursery staff that the building was far too easy to break into. They suggested that a burglar alarm should be installed and this way the vandals would be rumbled if they ever came back.

The local community in Scotswood were very shaken and upset by the death of Martin Brown. They arranged a campaign to improve safety in the areas where demolition and building work was taking place. These dangerous sites were no place for children. At this time the local community had no idea that Martin had been murdered. They assumed his death was a result of a lack of security and fencing at the derelict demolition sites. There were some protest marches and banners for this campaign and this resulted in the rare occurrence of a childhood photograph of Mary Bell captured for posterity. There is she, in a little coat, helping to hold up a banner demanding that Scotswood should be made safer for children. She's tiny and you can't see her face very well but it is definitely Mary Bell. This was a rare case of a killer staying at the scene of a crime and hiding in plain sight. Mary was eleven so she didn't have much choice about that but her chutzpah is astonishing. Mary Bell has murdered a child and then placed herself front and centre of a local campaign to protect children. Mary must have been feeling bullet proof at this time. This disturbed girl must have thought she could get away with anything.

SVENGALI

A few days before the funeral of Martin Brown, Mary Bell and Norma knocked on the door of his mother June and asked if they could see him. June quickly realised that the children meant they wanted to see him in his coffin. She told them to go away. June had only met Mary Bell a few times when Martin was alive but after his death she kept seeing Mary Bell all the time. June was not the only member of the family who was beginning to find Mary Bell irritating. Rita Finlay said that Mary and Norma kept turning up on her doorstep volunteering to look after her son John. Rita Finlay was June's older sister. Rita had ran to the derelict house after being informed of Martin's accident by Mary and Norma and a local woman. At the time Rita was preparing to cook the dinner for her family. She said she just dropped all the food on the floor and ran as fast as she could. When she'd reached the derelict house Mary Bell suddenly popped up outside. Mary Bell's determination to follow Rita around at this precise time to see her reaction was sick and horrible.

Though she never had much time for Mary Bell, Rita later described Norma as a lovely girl who she had a lot of affection for. Norma had a soft spot for Rita's little son John and was always kind to him. Norma would jokingly refer to John as her 'boyfriend'. Rita said that Mary and Norma washed John's hair and were a great help. She just thought they were being nice and trying to help her feel better after the tragedy. In the end though, Mary Bell constantly asked her questions about Martin's death to the point where Rita told Mary to go away and leave her alone. Mary literally could not shut up about the death of Martin Brown. She told other children that she had murdered him. Mary was aware that the children were not likely to take her at face value but she liked to say things like this to shock them. When she was in the home of the local Howe family, Mary hinted that she knew something which would get Norma locked up. Mary was falsely implying that Norma had something to do with Martin's death.

The Howe family was where Mary Bell's next victim came from. She would target the child of a family she was friends with and knew quite well. It is hard to say why she did this. She may have presumed that her familiarity with these families made her the last person who would be suspected of foul play. It could be the case that Mary was jealous of other families in the area with more loving and stable home environments than she ever enjoyed. This theory would propose that the murders were revenge for this envy. The more simple explanation is that Mary Bell enjoyed hurting children. The murder of Martin Brown was something she had enjoyed. Mary Bell would, many years later, say she had not intended to harm Martin Brown and did not know that her actions were dangerous. She said she presumed that Martin would wake up in the house and go home. This was not validated though by

Mary's conduct in the wake of the tragedy. She was well aware that Martin Brown was gone and not coming back and she took great delight in this knowledge. Mary Bell enjoyed all the community drama and sorrow which followed. She had the time of life attending protests and pestering the Brown family.

A large number of killers had unhappy childhoods. There are exceptions to this of course but many killers had an awful start in life. In many cases they experienced grim poverty or suffered abuse - or in many cases experienced both of these factors. It is by no means completely universal but a common thread between many murderers often seems to be a dysfunctional relationship with their mother. It seems to a recurring pattern too that many murderers were beaten and verbally abused by strict fathers. The 1988 publication Sexual Homicide, Patterns and Motives said that 70% of families who raised a serial killer have had a history of alcohol abuse. Some of this criteria applied to Mary Bell and some did not. Technically speaking, Mary Bell is not classified as a murderer because she was convicted of manslaughter. It seems a stretch though to say she wasn't a killer. You don't squeeze the neck of a much smaller and younger child and not expect something bad to happen. Mary Bell was eleven years old. She wasn't a toddler.

The day after Martin Brown's murder, Mary Bell had an altercation with Norma's sister Susan. Mary Bell began to throttle Susan but Norma's father noticed what was happening and gave Mary a 'clip' on the shoulder. Norma's parents were beginning to realise, not before time, that little May Bell from number 70 was not a very good influence on their daughter. Norma's mother Catherine later testified in court that she had witnessed Mary Bell tried to strangle her daughter Susan. Catherine Bell had no great love for Mary - especially by the time of the murder trial. By that stage Catherine was well aware that Mary Bell was going down and intent on dragging Norma with her. Mary seemed incapable of getting along with other children so her friendship with Norma was atypical and of great value to her. This did not though stop Mary from trying to pin the murders on Norma when she ended up in hot water with the police.

It would later come to light that in her school notebook Mary had drawn a picture of a boy lying on the floor next to a bottle of tablets. Mary had also drawn a workman (with pickaxe) arriving to find the body. Next to the picture she had written (complete with spelling errors), "On saturday I was in the house, and my mam sent Me to ask Norma if she Would come up the top with me? we went up and we came down at Magrets Road and there were crowds of people beside an old house. I asked what was the matter. there had been a boy who Just lay down and Died." Mary's teacher, while obviously not suspecting Mary of anything, did think it was slightly strange that Mary Bell was the only pupil who had written about Martin Brown in her notebook. Mary Bell was not the only person who was excited by all the local community drama surrounding the death of Martin Brown. Norma was also excited by this activity and all the gossip and theories. Norma was still blissfully unaware that Mary had blamed her for the murder in at least one household. When they visited the house where Martin Brown's family lived to ask questions or simply make an appearance, Mary and Norma were actually playing a private game of 'chicken' where they dared one another to do things like ask about Martin's coffin.

There are few photographs of Norma Joyce Bell online. In the most common one she has dark eyes, is wearing a checked shirt, has a lopsided fringe and greasy black hair, and the signs of some acne or blotchy skin. Norma is not unattractive though and actually very pretty in a slightly unconventional way. Norma has a blank expression in the photograph and doesn't appear to be the sort of child with a ready smile. From what we know of Norma she was an uncomplicated girl at heart who found it easy to make friends. If she had been born somewhere else, somewhere far away from Mary Bell, her early life would have been a lot more uneventful and happy. At the trial Mary Bell was accused of having a 'Svengali' influence over Norma. Svengali is a term that originates from George du Maurier's 1894 novel Trilby. In the story, Svengali is a charismatic and manipulative musician who exerts an overwhelming influence over the titular character, Trilby, turning her into a famous singer. The term has since come to indicate any person who manipulates or controls another person, typically for their own benefit.

Mary's influence over Norma has probably been slightly exaggerated in the snowballing of this horrible tale. Mary was the sharper of the two and the more willing to look for trouble but Norma wasn't dragged along on this ride because she had no choice. She did have a choice. She didn't have to vandalise a nursery or torment Martin Brown's family. Norma chose to do these things because Mary Bell was her friend and she enjoyed Mary's company. Norma got a kick out of Mary Bell. She enjoyed that danger of doing 'naughty' things. It was really a question of how far Norma would be willing to follow Mary so long as this unhealthy friendship continued to flourish. Mary Bell is often called a master of manipulation in retrospectives of her life and crimes. Manipulation is certainly a trait which we've seen in many notorious killers. They often have a surface charm which allows them (for a time at least) to avoid suspicion. Aside from Norma though there wasn't much evidence of Mary manipulating anyone and her control over Norma was not as total as is sometimes made out.

We saw evidence of this when Norma 'ratted' on Mary Bell in her police statement after the sandpit attack. Norma's statement did not suggest someone who was completely dominated by her friend. There wasn't much evidence of Mary Bell having any charm or likeable qualities either. Though she was said to have a good sense of humour most people who knew her remembered Mary Bell as a sullen child who always looked annoyed about something. The experts who later interviewed Mary Bell when she was locked up generally came to the conclusion that she was a psychopath. Psychopaths engage in risky or reckless behaviour without considering the consequences, and they often struggle with maintaining responsibilities. They lack empathy and struggle to connect to others. This is what made Norma unique in that she had formed a close friendship with Mary. There was no real motivation for Mary Bell's murders. The victims had not angered or wronged her in any way. Mary had nothing to gain from the murders in the way of theft or money. They were just senseless acts of evil. Mary Bell was simply curious to see what it would be like to take a life and afterwards she was completely unaffected. She either didn't seem to understand the gravity of what she had done or she didn't care.

Whitehouse Road, where Mary and Norma lived, was part of a council estate north of Scotswood Road and looked like a Victorian gothic version of Coronation Street. The dark connected houses (some of which were divided into flats) looked bleak, jagged, and on the brink of falling over. There were some banks of grass and little footpaths behind the houses. Whitehouse Road was perched on a hill and had clear views of the city. The area had suffered from the decline in industrial jobs (which began in the 1950s) and by the time of Mary Bell's childhood, Scotswood had one of the worst crime and unemployment rates in England. Mary slept in a room at 70 Whitehouse Road which was previously used to store coal. In those days most people had a coal fire so there was plenty of chimney smoke and soot in the air. Mary Bell later recalled that a friend of Billy sometimes stayed in the house and also a woman who wasn't related to them. This indicates that Betty Bell might have had a lodger.

Mary often stayed over with relatives due to Billy and Betty not always being at home. This gave Mary a rootless sort of feeling as if she didn't belong to anyone. With this in mind we can see how important Norma was to Mary Bell. Norma was Mary's main connection to the world. They spent a lot of time together in Mary's room or outside and had fantasies of running away together. These fantasies seemed real to Mary. The sense of dislocation Mary Bell experienced as a child and the ill treatment of her by Betty (like trying to give Mary away) was clearly a factor in the way Mary Bell turned out. She wasn't just born evil. That doesn't completely explain what she did and it most definitely doesn't mitigate it in any way. The most alarming trait in Mary Bell before the events of 1968 was her anger. Mary could snap in an instant and suddenly attack another child in a frenzy for no reason. The murders were different. Mary was calm and controlled when she killed.

Mary and Norma, unaware that a burglar alarm had been fitted, decided to break into the Woodlands Crescent nursery again on the 31st of May for another bout of vandalism. This time the alarm was triggered and Mary and Norma were detained so that the police could talk to them. This was the third time the local police had interviewed Mary and Norma and it certainly wouldn't be the last. The two girls lied and told the police that this was the first time they had broken into the nursery and said they knew nothing about the previous vandalism incident or the strange notes which were left. The police (who you would imagine didn't believe Mary and Norma's story) didn't take the matter much further. They had far more important crimes to investigate than nursery break ins by young girls. Mary and Norma were charged with breaking and entering but it wasn't treated as a very serious crime and they didn't get into that much trouble. Norma's parents must have been very disappointed with her and increasingly worried about her friendship with Mary Bell. The only consolation for them was the knowledge that childhood friends tend to drift apart in the end. They must have hoped this would happen sooner rather than later.

By now Martin Brown had been buried. Shamefully, his family was denied the compensation required to get him a proper headstone. June Brown's life would never be the same again but she had to carry on for the sake of her other children. She was unaware that Martin's tragic death, which was now slipping out of the local news, would soon be the basis of national headlines and a very strange trial. Meanwhile, Mary and Norma continued to hang around together all the time, looking for ways to cause mischief to amuse themselves. Mary was disappointed that all the drama surrounding Martin's death was beginning to calm down. What seemed to motivate Mary was that she was in possession of knowledge that no one else had. She knew how Martin died but no one else did. Not the Brown family nor the police or public. Mary Bell enjoyed having this secret but it was of no use to her if she couldn't talk about it.

This is what inspired the notes left at the nursery and this is what made Mary tell children that she had killed Martin Brown. Mary was aware that this secret was bad news for her if fully disclosed but she felt it was safe to be cryptic or simply say it to children - who would tell no one and not be believed even if they did. If a child told their mother or father that little May Bell from Whitehouse Road had confessed to being a murderer that parent was not going to take it seriously. Mary felt it was safe then to play these games. She was safe too. No one in Scotswood, including the police, were aware that Martin Brown had been murdered. No one suspected Mary Bell of being anything other than a strange child who was always getting into fights. The only way this situation could change was if foul play was established in relation to Martin Brown but that ship seemed to have sailed now. The only other way Mary Bell's situation could potentially change for the worse was if she did the same thing again to another child. Tragically, this was a gamble that Mary Bell could not resist and was willing to take.

Mary Bell murdered a child for the second time on the 31st of July 1968. The victim was three year-old Brian Howe. Rita Finlay, the aunt of Martin Brown, knew Brian Howe very well because he was best friends with her son John. The last time Brian's parents saw him he was playing in the street with his siblings and Mary and Norma. Brian ended up going to the 'Tin Lizzie' waste ground with Mary and Norma and it was here where his life ended. The Tin Lizzie was not quite as you might imagine it to be. The Mary Bell case makes it seem like some enclosed private space full of building supplies. In reality it was quite bumpy, bleak, and windswept with big patches of open ground. There were houses in the background too. The murder followed a similar pattern to that of Martin Brown. Mary allowed a young child to tag along with her to an isolated spot and then attacked them. The big difference this time is that Norma was there too. It later transpired that Mary and Norma had discussed killing children together as a sort of fantasy. It was no fantasy to Mary Bell though but something she did in reality. As far as Norma was concerned it was a fantasy. She was not capable of murder. Nonetheless, the conduct of Norma in this second tragic incident was baffling, criminal, and unpleasant. Norma was thirteen years old. She was a teenager. She wasn't a little kid who didn't know better.

When they got to the Tin Lizzie, Mary told Brian he had a sore throat and she would rub it for him. Mary began to strangle Brian much as she done with Martin Brown. Norma did not do anything to help Brian. She just stood there and watched. There was a group of boys playing nearby but Norma did not shout for help nor did she (despite being bigger and older) pull Mary off Brian. Norma later insisted she never touched Brian and it was all Mary Bell's doing. Norma was telling the truth when she said this but her inaction contributed to Brian's death. She was in a position to save him but did nothing. The only defence Norma offered was to say she had no idea that Mary was going to attack Brian and Brian was alive when she left. It all happened too quickly to take in. Mary and Norma departed together - leaving Brian Howe dead by cement blocks and oil drums in the Tin Lizzie. But they returned at least twice to look at the body again. There was also evidence of crude mutilation of Brian's genitals and stomach.

There were cuts to Brian's legs and a few puncture marks. Some of his hair had been snipped off. A letter was carved into his stomach. It looked like an M but could have been an N. Norma denied she took part in these grisly activities but certainly went back with Mary Bell to look at the body. Brian was reported missing by his family. His mother Eileen was not living at home at the time so Brian's guardian was his much older sister Pat. Mary and Norma went to find Pat and asked if she was looking for Brian. Pat said she was and they took her to the Tin Lizzie and explained this was where all the kids went to play. Mary Bell was trying to usher Pat towards the place where Brian was. Mary wanted to see Pat's reaction when she found Brian. This malicious and chilling ruse told you all you needed to know about Mary Bell. Pat did not find Brian's body in the end because she did not want to search the entire area on her own. She decided to call the police. The police had torches and dogs and found Brian's body at 11-10 pm. There was evidence of a very childlike and pointless attempt to hide the body by throwing some tufts of grass and weed over it.

The inquest into Martin Brown's death had been recorded an open verdict. It was very different this time. There were 'pinch' marks on Brian's nose and abrasions to his throat. The post mortem established that he had been suffocated. There were the mutilations to his body too. The police found a pair of rusty scissors at the crime scene which may have been used for these crude mutilations. The medical examination determined that while Brian had been suffocated the nature of the injuries indicated that the assailant had been someone of minimal strength. The verdict of the medical examiner was shocking. His report stated that the person who murdered Brian was probably a child. It was the only explanation that made sense. The police now had to reconsider the death of Martin Brown - who had died in the same area just a few months ago. Martin was almost the same age of Brian. His death suddenly no longer looked like an unexplained accident.

The police eventually realised that these cases had to be connected. This was bad news for Mary Bell because the two victims had something else in common. The last time either of them were seen alive they were seen with her. You can see then that Mary Bell wasn't very bright. She had got away with the murder of Martin Brown and if she hadn't killed again no one would have known what really happened. But by committing another identical murder in the same area so soon afterwards, Mary had more or less sealed her own fate. The focus of the police investigation was on the children in the Scotswood area. The police talked to hundreds of children and established that the last time Brian Howe was seen alive he was with Mary and Norma. The police also learned from Brian's sister Pat that Mary and Norma seemed to know the precise spot where Brian would be found.

CID (Criminal Investigation Department) detective Harvey Burrows and Detective-Chief-Inspector James Dobson both become oddly suspicious of Mary Bell while conducting investigations in the area because she seemed strangely intent on following the case at close hand, often following police officers around to see where they were going. Dobson said that when the coffin of Brian Howe was brought out of the house for the funeral he noticed Mary Bell laughing to herself amid a group of onlookers and people paying their respects. By this time the police had a number of statements from children saying that they'd last seen Brian Howe playing with Mary and Norma. Mary and Norma were therefore brought in to answer some questions on the 1st of August. In situations like this Mary was often supported by other relatives due to Betty and Billy not always being at home. Mary Bell was not especially concerned or nervous because by now she was used to give police statements and interviews. She was also used to getting away with anything she did without any punishment. Mary didn't seem to believe there was much chance of her being a suspect in this case.

Mary and Norma, as was their custom, managed to dovetail their statement surprisingly well. They were both released after their statements. Both of them told the police they had seen Brian on the day he died and played with him for a while.

Mary and Norma both said too though that after they had their lunch they never saw Brian again. So the basic timeline they gave the police was that they hadn't seen Brian again in the afternoon. This was a promising start for Mary Bell but she then made a colossal mistake. This mistake starkly illustrated once again that Mary was an eleven year-old child of very average intelligence and not the cunning Machiavellian criminal genius that retrospective articles sometimes make her out to be. Mary decided that, to throw the police off her scent, she would give them an alternative suspect. The person she chose was an eight year-old boy (this boy was never named in public) who often played on the Tin Lizzie. Mary told the police she saw this boy with Brian the day of the Brian's death. Mary also said she had seen the boy strike Brian. She wasn't quite finished yet. Mary also informed the police that the boy was carrying a pair of scissors which were slightly bent at the handle.

The only people who knew about the twisted scissors found at the murder scene were police detectives. The scissors had never been disclosed to newspapers or the public. Detective-Chief-Inspector James Dobson already had his suspicions about Mary Bell and these suspicions were now confirmed. Mary Bell could only know about those scissors if she had been at the crime scene before the police found Brian. The only other alternative was that Mary was telling the truth and the boy she was now casting as a suspect had been the person who left the scissors at the crime scene. The police now needed to talk to the boy Mary had named and establish his movements on the day Brian was murdered. The boy in question was actually at Newcastle airport with family the afternoon of the murder. His movements on the day of the murder were painstakingly investigated and verified by the police and it was proven that it would have been impossible for him to have been the person who harmed Brian Howe. Mary Bell's attempt to frame this boy for the murder was quickly exposed as a complete lie. She had completely shot herself in the foot because now the police knew she couldn't be trusted and wasn't telling the truth.

WORSE THAN HARRY ROBERTS

On the 4th of August the police were told by Norma's family that she had a confession to make. Norma's parents were well aware this was becoming very serious and they were desperate to extract Norma from this investigation and leave Mary Bell to her own fate. They didn't believe Norma had anything to do with Brian Howe's death and were very annoyed and worried at the thought of their daughter getting a share of the blame for whatever terrible things Mary Bell had done. Detective-Chief-Inspector James Dobson went to see Norma and managed to talk to her alone. Norma told Mr Dobson that Mary had taken her to see Brian Howe's body. She said that Mary had told her about the murder and how she did it. Norma told Mr Dobson that after confessing to the murder Mary Bell had warned her to keep her mouth shut. Norma said that she tripped over Brian Howe's body when Mary took her there because she hadn't expected it to be there. Norma said Mary had used a razor, which she hid on the Tin Lizzie under a block of cement, to cut Brian's belly. Norma also said Mary had confessed to her that she had enjoyed carrying out the murder and might kill again in the future.

Detective-Chief-Inspector Dobson took Norma out to the Tin Lizzie to see if she could show him where Brian was found. Norma did this and also showed him the hidden razor that Mary had used. Once this was done, Norma was taken back to the police station to make a statement. Norma was not yet telling the complete truth though because she hadn't confessed to the police that she was present when Brian was murdered. Norma now made an official statement to the police in relation to what she knew about Brian Howe. She was made aware that any statement was her own choice and could used in evidence against her. Norma's family had obviously told her she had to make the statement. In her statement Norma (who referred to Mary Bell as May throughout) said that she had tagged along with Mary Bell when Mary took her dog for a walk and Mary had then (to Norma's surprise) taken her to the body of Brian Howe. Norma described what she saw. Brian's eyes were open and lips were purple. He was covered in dirt. Mary showed Norma how she had killed him by pinching his neck. She then show Norma the razor and the cuts on Brian. Norma said they left the scene in a rush because there was a man quite near to them calling out to a child.

Norma referred to the Tin Lizzie waste ground as 'the blocks' in her statement. This is what the local kids tended to call it. To get to the cement block area, Mary and Norma had to go through a car park and find a hole in a fence. Norma said in her statement that after parting with Mary she went and played with some other kids - all of whom she named. She didn't see Mary again until about a quarter to seven. Mary was with Brian's sister Pat and had agreed to help look for Brian. Norma said she also agreed to help search. Norma said that Mary Bell told Pat that Brian might be up at 'the blocks' and they should look there. However, Pat decided to stop the search at seven o'clock and phone the police. Norma said that she then went to the home of her friend Linda Routledge until half past eight before going home. This was the general nature of Norma's statement though there were other details too. Norma said Mary told her she wasn't frightened by dead bodies because she had seen one before. Norma told the police in her statement that she hadn't 'snitched' on Mary straight away because she was frightened that Mary might snatch another 'bairn' if she did that. That last part of the statement didn't make much sense but, in general terms, Norma's statement was credible and didn't have any obvious contradictions.

On the 5th of August the police went to 70 Whitehouse Road to fetch Mary Bell and take her to the police station for an interview. Detective-Chief-Inspector James Dobson and Inspector Larry Laggan were the officers tasked with this duty. When they got the house it was the evening and Mary Bell had gone to bed. Betty Bell was not home but Billy Bell was still up watching television. Billy, who for obvious reasons was wary of police officers, wouldn't let them in at first but eventually opened the door when they explained what this was all about. Billy went to find his sister Audrey (who lived nearby) to take Mary to the station. The police said that Billy Bell identified himself as Mary's uncle rather than her father. At the police station Mary Bell was questioned by James Dobson. Mr Dobson said Mary was an odd girl and described her as a 'kook'. Mary Bell told Mr Dobson that she knew nothing about Brian Howe's death and stuck to that line rigidly. Sometimes she would respond to a question with complete silence.

Mr Dobson asked Mary Bell if she thought it was wrong to squeeze a little boy's throat. "Worse than Harry Roberts," replied Mary. Harry Roberts was a criminal and murderer who in 1966 instigated the Shepherd's Bush murders, in which three police officers were shot dead in London. Mr Dobson asked Mary about the man who Norma said had shouted close by when they visited the body of Brian Howe. Mr Dobson suggested to Mary that this man would recognise her if he was brought in by the police. Mary responded by saying he would need good eyesight to recognise her because she wasn't even there. Mary accused Detective-Chief-Inspector Dobson of trying to 'brainwash' her and said she was tired of making statements for things she hadn't done. She told Dobson that Norma was a liar always trying to get her into trouble. At this stage in the investigation, the police didn't know about the nursery sandpit incident where Mary had tried to strangle two little girls. Odd as it may sound, the police detectives investigating the death of Brian Howe had also yet to work out that Mary and Norma were connected to the nursery vandalism incident where macabre notes in relation to Martin Brown were left.

Detective-Chief-Inspector James Dobson still had to retain an open mind at this early stage. He hadn't completely ruled out the possibility that Norma was the dangerous one out of the two girls and that her statement was a carefully crafted fiction designed to shift the blame to Mary. A few days later though came the incident where Mr Dobson noticed Mary Bell laughing and joking as the coffin of Brian Howe was taken from his home to prepare for the funeral. There was something very weird and unsettling about this girl that Mr Dobson didn't like at all. Norma Joyce Bell was taken to Fernwood Remand Home by the police so that she could focus on giving them evidence with no distractions. The translation of this is they wanted Norma to have no contact with Mary Bell. Fernwood Remand Home is a Victorian building, located in Newcastle upon Tyne. It used to be a maternity hospital but was purchased by the local council and turned into a children's home in the 1960s. These days, Fernwood is the head office of Lowes Financial Management. Fernwood Remand Home was where Mary Bell was later housed during her trial.

Norma, after consulting with her family, requested the chance to make another police statement. She said some important details were left out of her last statement and she wanted to rectify that. The police were more than happy to get more information. One of the reasons why they had isolated Norma and placed her in the care of the children's home is that they wanted to assess her character and get a closer look at Norma in order to work out if she was telling

40

the truth. Norma was very different in police interviews than Mary Bell. Norma seemed fascinated by the whole process and was friendly and polite. Mary on the other hand was sullen and made no attempt to conceal her anger and irritation at being forced to go to the police station. The main purpose of Norma's fresh statement was to confess to the police that she had been present when Brian Howe died. This was something (that Norma was present but had nothing to do with the murder) her parents must have dragged out of her and told her she must tell the police before they deduced it for themselves. It wouldn't look good for Norma if she was found to be lying about her exact whereabouts when Brian died.

Norma read her statement aloud to police detectives and it was written down. She asked that her parents not be present - only police officers. Norma said that on the day of the murder she was out with Mary Bell and in the afternoon, about three, they saw Brian Howe playing with his brother and others. Norma said that Brian's brother gave him a pair of scissors. Brian then went off with Mary and Norma and Norma took the scissors and kept them in her pocket (it appears that both the scissors and the razor were used by Mary Bell when she cut the body). Norma's new statement claimed that she, Mary, and Brian Howe had gone for a walk and initially tried to get in a rusted water tank - which they abandoned because it was too smelly. Mary had then suggested they go to 'the blocks' (the Tin Lizzie) so they ended up there. Norma said that Mary then began to strangle Brian. Brian struggled but he wasn't strong enough. He fell to the ground gasping. Norma said Mary had gone all 'funny' and was now deranged. Norma told the police she told Mary to stop but Mary ignored her. She strangled Brian again and then suggested that Norma take over. Norma said she ran away at this point and went back to Whitehouse Road. Before she did this she dropped the scissors she had been carrying.

Norma told the police that Mary came and found her about twenty minutes later. They then back to the cement blocks where Brian was. Norma said she knew he was dead after she checked his pulse. Norma said that Mary produced the razor and cut Brian's stomach. Norma said they returned to Whitehouse Road but after having their tea went back to the Tin Lizzie. Mary cut Brian's body again - this time with the scissors. She also cut off a lock of Brian's hair. The two girls then heard some boys not far away so fled and went home. The next time Norma saw Mary was when she was with Pat Howe and volunteering to look for Brian. It was certainly a shrewd move by Norma and her family to quickly produce a second statement confessing to having been present when Brian died. Fibres from the clothes worn by Mary Bell and Norma were found on Brian's body by the police forensics team so the police would have found this out themselves in the end. Norma's statement was unbearably sad and unpleasant. Even if she hadn't participated in the murder she still didn't come out of this very well. She failed to protect Brian and then returned on two occasions to gawp at the body.

If Norma's family thought that her honesty would be enough to get her off the hook they were to be disappointed. Norma had admitted to being present when a child died. This demanded further scrutiny. The police couldn't just take Norma's word that it was all Mary and she didn't lay a finger on Brian. The police took Norma out to the Tin Lizzie two more times just to make certain that her statements were credible when it came to routes and directions. They also compared the descriptions by Norma of marks Mary (according to Norma) had made on Brian's body with a medical examination of the deceased victim. Norma's descriptions matched the actual cuts and puncture marks on the body. So once again, Norma's statement was credible - only this time with more detail. The only thing which remained unclear was whether Norma was telling the truth about Mary being the only one who had harmed Brian. The next step for the police was to talk to Mary Bell again. This was something that Mary Bell must have been anticipating with a large degree of dread.

When the police arrived at Mary's house there were no adults at home. The police therefore took all of the Bell children to the police station. Mary's siblings were given something to eat and toys to play with while they questioned Mary in another room. Detective-Chief-Inspector Dobson said it was a very different Mary Bell who sat down in the police station for her second round of questioning. She was more nervous this time and the confident defiance was no longer quite so evident. Mary was required to give her own police statement on what had happened. Mr Dobson had to telephone the hospital and get a nurse to come and sit with Mary during the interview because it was against the law for a female child under sixteen to make a police statement about a serious crime without a neutral adult of the same sex being in the room to look after them. The police were very interested to see how much this statement would differ from the one recently given by Norma Joyce Bell.

Mary's statement began with her and Norma in the street and then running into Brian Howe. Mary said that Norma asked Brian if he wanted to come to the shop with them. Mary said she thought this was strange because Norma didn't have any money. Mary claimed that she wanted Brian to go home but Norma refused to let Brian leave. Mary's statement was suffused with little details designed to cast Norma in a bad light. Mary said that, as they walked, Norma was racist towards a black boy and tried to start a fight with him. Then she said that Norma promised Brian they were going to see a nice old lady who had some sweets. Mary said they got in an old water tank to look at some tadpoles. Norma said Brian had a sore throat and started to squeeze his neck but then she stopped. After this, Norma told Brian they needed to go to 'the blocks' because that was where the old lady with the sweets was waiting. At the blocks, Mary said Norma instructed Brian to lay down. Mary claimed that Norma then began to strangle Brian with such intent that her fingers turned down white.

Mary told the police that she tried to stop Norma by grabbing her shoulders but Norma shrugged her off and then turned around and screamed at her. Mary went on to say that by this point Brian had banged his head on something and had turned white and blue with a frothing mouth. Norma (according to Mary's statement) covered him with a coat. Mary said she told Norma she wouldn't tell on her because she was frightened of Norma (Mary Bell completely - and stupidly - contradicted this part of the police statement during the trial when she said she wasn't scared of Norma and would have 'belted her one' if Norma had ever threatened her). Mary's next flourish in her police statement was to add that Brian's dog had followed them and Norma tried to strangle the dog too but had to abandon this because the dog growled at her. One can see here that parts of Mary Bell's statement were a lot more fantastical and childlike than Norma's statement. It was far less credible in places. Mary Bell was supposed to be the clever one in this double act but she wasn't doing herself too many favours so far.

Mary said she then took Brian's dog home. Norma, according to Mary, had gone into a sort of trance and was making 'funny' faces. Norma said this wasn't the first time she had killed and wouldn't be the last. Mary said Norma then went home to get some scissors and they went back to the 'blocks' where the body of Brian was. Norma had a razor too and tried to cut Brian's ear and stomach. She cut off some of his hair too. Mary said Norma demonstrated the sharpness of the razor by cutting a piece of her cotton dress. When she was finished, Norma left the razor under a block and put the scissors next to Brian. Mary then took the time in her statement to say she didn't have the 'guts' to do the horrible things which Norma did. Mary said she wouldn't even be capable of harming a bird. Mary said she was crying by this point in anguish over what Norma had done. She said she warned Norma that Pat Howe would kill her if she found out what had happened.

Mary said that when she helped Pat look for Brian later on she was trying to direct Pat to where Brian's body was to be kind and bring about a resolution. Mary said that Norma ruined this act of 'kindness' by telling Pat not to look in 'the blocks'. Mary's statement ended by saying that she went home about half seven and when she woke up the next day Brian had been found. Mary said that Norma wanted to go on the run and move from children's home to children's home because that way she could murder children and never get caught. Mary said in her statement she had declined Norma's offer to run away with her. Mary's police statement often read a lot like Norma's statement only flipped on its head with Norma as the killer rather than Mary. Much is made in the Mary Bell story of the intense dysfunctional bond between Mary and Norma but in the end that bond proved to be surprisingly flimsy and artificial. Norma was always more than willing to 'rat' on Mary's misdeeds. She had no real loyalty to Mary Bell. Mary had even less regard for Norma. Once she sensed the police were homing in on her for the death of Brian Howe, Mary wasted no time in pretending that Norma was the killer.

On the 8th of August, Mary and Norma were both charged with the murder of Brian Howe. The authorities decided it would be up to a court to decide which of the girls was lying and which was telling the truth - or if both girls were lying and equally guilty. By the time of the trial they would also be charged with the death of Martin Brown. The authorities learned a lot more in the months after Brian Howe's death.

They learned of the nursery break in and Mary trying to strangle two girls in the sandpit. They learned of the incident where a young boy was found badly injured after being in the company of Mary and Norma. They learned of Mary Bell's school notebook illustration of Martin Brown lying in the derelict house. All of this was very bad news for Mary Bell. It made her look like a disturbed child very much capable of fatally harming young children. It wasn't looking very good for Norma either because she was joined at the hip with Mary Bell throughout most of these events.

NATURE v NURTURE

Mary Bell was phlegmatic when she learned she was to be charged with murder. She said that was fine by her. Mary Bell didn't seem to understand the situation she now faced was very serious and would have profound ramifications for her entire life. She had a childlike expectation that this pickle would be over soon and she would be allowed to go home and resume her normal daily life. If you had told the eleven year-old Mary Bell in 1968 that she would now be locked up until 1980 (which would have sounded like an impossible far off futuristic year to a little kid in 1968) it is highly doubtful she would have been able to comprehend or imagine that. Norma Joyce Bell did not take the news of her murder charge as calmly as Mary Bell. Norma was angry and upset. She was furious. Norma swore revenge on Mary Bell. Norma, although usually portrayed as dim-witted and clueless in the Mary Bell story, was well aware of what Mary was doing. Mary Bell was trying to frame Norma for the murders. Mary was intent on doing as much damage to Norma as possible because she saw it as her only way to avoid being blamed for the murders. The fact that Norma was innocent of any murders was irrelevant to Mary. She didn't care. Mary's desired scenario was that

Norma would be locked up for the murders while she would walk free and go home to play with her dog and watch television.

Mary and Norma had to sleep in the police station that night because appropriate accommodation was still being arranged for them. The girls would obviously have to go to separate places and not have any contact before the trial. That night in the cells was the swansong for the Mary/Norma relationship. They would see one another at the trial but the night in the police station was the last time they ever directly spoke to each other in their lives. The pair were in surprisingly high spirits and the animosity between them seemed to be temporarily forgotten. The curious situation of being in a police station seemed exciting to Mary and Norma. They even sang some songs. The police officers in the station had to get the two girls some fish & chips so they would have something to eat for their dinner. The police officers couldn't help feeling a bit sorry for these two girls and protective of them. They brought Mary and Norma a bag of apples to eat too. Mary and Norma were then given fresh blankets and went to sleep in separate cells. They must have felt like the outlaws they sometimes used to fantasise about becoming. It was difficult for the police officers to get their head around the awful things these two girls were accused of. Mary and Norma seemed like harmless and normal children that night.

Martin Brown and Brian Howe were buried at St John's Cemetery in Elswick. Their lives were over before they had even begun. Mary Bell and Norma had not displayed any sadness or emotion over these tragic deaths. Mary Bell had actually enjoyed both the murders and the aftermath. She seemed to regard the whole thing as an exciting and atypical chapter in her otherwise humdrum life. Norma was innocent of harming the children but she'd still gone to look at the body of Brian Howe twice and then headed home to play with other children and have her tea. She had displayed all the emotion of someone who had found an expired mouse the cat brought into the kitchen. In fact, someone who found an expired mouse in their kitchen would probably have had more of a reaction that Norma did at viewing a dead body. These two girls were not normal. Mary was much worse than Norma but there was something deeply wrong with both of them.

Now that the two girls were in custody it quickly became apparent that Norma had a more responsive family unit than Mary. The authorities found it difficult to locate Betty Bell whereas Norma's parents were always there for their daughter and offered her constant support during this period. Mary did at least have the support of her aunts and grandmother, all of whom were good responsible people. Billy Bell was also a comfort to Mary Bell. Though he was surely no role model for any child he visited Mary when he could and stood by her. Brian Howe's mother Eileen Corrigan had to use sedatives after Brian's death to cope with the pain of the loss. Her marriage ended and she moved. One of her sons was taken into care because she couldn't cope. The person responsible for all of this was Mary Bell. Mary Bell had shattered Eileen Corrigan's life into a million pieces but Mary was completely oblivious to this. Even if you'd sat Mary Bell down and this explained this to her she wouldn't have cared. Mary Bell had laughed when she saw the Howe family leaving the house for the funeral. She thought this tragedy was great fun.

Martin Brown's mother, who became June Richardson, also saw her marriage collapse. She started drinking too much and lost her faith in people. June stopped her kids (she had an infant daughter when Martin died and another daughter later) from playing with other kids because she didn't trust children anymore. She wouldn't let children in the house and got nervous when her kids had to go to school. June said she became full of hate. She never got over Martin's death. It was only the arrival of her first grandchild that made June let go of the hate. June said her coping mechanism was to not think about Mary Bell anymore. She liked to think that Mary Bell was dead. June said her marriage ended because she and her husband George simply made each think of Martin. This was so painful that they had no option but to part. They say that time is a great healer but this wasn't really the case for June. Bereavement was like a scar to June. It faded but it was always there and sometimes it would open again and become painful.

When she learned about Martin's 'accident', June had ran to the house where they found him. She was in the ambulance with Martin as they unsuccessfully tried to revive him. June had to view Martin's body to officially identify him after his death. His face still had sawdust on it from lying in the old house. June requested that no one else from the family view the body because she didn't want them to go through that. June later said she always had some doubts about whether Martin's death was really an accident. Martin was found in a room that needed three flights of stairs to reach. June thought this was odd because Martin was always scared of stairs due to falling down the ones at home once.

There was something about his death that didn't quite add up. It seemed so random and unexplained. There were no answers. The reason for this would become shockingly apparent

in the wake of Brian Howe's death. It was not lost on June that a painful and tragic detail in this case is that another child had to die for the truth about Martin's death to come out. Mary Bell had more or less committed the 'perfect murder' with Martin Brown. She had completely got away with it. The murder of Brian Howe was different.

Psychiatrists who treated Mary Bell in custody judged her to be suffering from what is called psychopathic personality disorder. Psychopathic personality disorder, often referred to simply as psychopathy, is displayed by a specific set of emotional, interpersonal, and behavioural traits. Individuals with this disorder usually exhibit a lack of empathy, guilt, or remorse, coupled with superficial charm, manipulativeness, and a tendency towards deceitfulness. They may also demonstrate impulsive behaviour, irresponsibility, and a shallow range of emotions. Psychopathy is distinct from other personality disorders and has been linked to both genetic and environmental factors.

Mary Bell had ticked a fair number of these boxes already and she had only just turned eleven years-old. She had shown no guilt or remorse (if anything she had displayed the complete opposite - glee) and impulsive criminal behaviour with no thought to the consequences was now a staple theme in her life.

After her night at the police station it was arranged for Mary Bell to be housed at a remand home in Seaham. Before this decision was taken she had been evaluated at an assessment centre in Croydon. A remand home is a facility that houses young individuals who are awaiting a court appearance or who have been committed by a court for specific reasons, often related to offenses or legal issues. These homes are typically intended for juveniles and serve as a secure environment while the youth's case is processed through the legal system. Seaham is a coastal town located situated on the North Sea and is part of the larger metropolitan borough of County Durham. Historically, Seaham developed as a port town in the 19th century, primarily due to coal mining and its proximity to the sea, which facilitated trade and transportation. The remand home at Seaham was run by a matron. The matron was a decent and fair woman who, so long as you abided by the rules, was almost like a grandmother figure to the girls housed there.

Mary Bell was younger than the other girls at Seaham but she didn't have any major problems there besides one incident where she had a scuffle with a girl who had called her mother a prostitute. The girl in question was on the money when it came to Betty Bell's occupation but Mary was in no mood to be reminded of her mother's line of work.

Living at Seaham was a lot nicer than living at number 70 Whitehouse Road. There were pretty gardens and sea views. The police said that when they went to Whitehouse Road to take Mary Bell away for questioning they were astonished and depressed by how empty Mary Bell's house was. It was literally an empty, cold, dark and dilapidated husk. Betty Bell had made no effort to turn it into anything resembling a home. Seaham was like living in a holiday resort by comparison. Mary Bell had got a temporary upgrade in her accommodation but there were disadvantages. She missed her dog and siblings. Mary Bell was aware by now that she had been plucked out of society but she didn't know where this was all leading. The concept of a trial and further punishment was still abstract in her mind.

Norma Joyce Bell was sent to Prudhoe Monkton Mental Hospital in Northumberland. This institution was housed at what used to be called Prudhoe Hall. It was situated in pleasant countryside surroundings and was basically a mental institution designed in the 'continental' style with plenty of space. There was a children's village for young inmates and little villas for the patients. By the time Norma went there it was one of the largest mental hospitals in the United Kingdom. Much of the site closed in 2005 and it became quite derelict in the end. Prudhoe had a walled garden and Victorian glasshouses and would have been a busy place when Norma was housed there. Norma already had a barrister and her parents visited her all the time. The people around Norma were confident that her innocence would be proven in court and Mary Bell would be left to carry the can.

Norma was judged to have the intelligence of an eight year-old in IQ tests at Prudhoe. She certainly wasn't Einstein. There are different types of intelligence though and so far Norma had handled her situation as well as could be expected. A lot of the credit for this went to her parents. Not only had they sensibly made Norma volunteer a second police statement and confess to being present at Brian Howe's murder they had also moved fast to hire a QC for their daughter. Norma going to Prudhoe was part of her bail condition. Norma's parents, on the advice of R.P Smith QC, agreed that if granted bail Norma would spend some time in a mental hospital. The term 'mental hospital' didn't have the same stigma back then that it does today. Back then it was just seen as a logical extension of the NHS. These days if you say the term 'mental hospital' you immediately tend to have images of rubber rooms and serial killers - which is of course misleading and simplistic.

Mary and Norma had to attend a remand hearing at the juvenile court in Newcastle. Billy Bell and Mary's grandmother turned up at this hearing but Betty Bell was absent. It turned out she was in Glasgow. The social services in Newcastle actually arranged for some staff to travel to Glasgow and remind Betty that her daughter was currently in custody awaiting a murder trial. Betty Bell didn't seem to have grasped this fact. It took over a week for Betty Bell to visit Mary at Seaham. Mary welcomed this visit despite the fact that her mother was angry with her for getting into this mess and dragging the family's name through the mud. Betty Bell did not believe that her daughter was a child murderer. She couldn't bring herself to accept this could possibly be true. This is a common theme in true crime cases. The mothers of killers are always the last to accept that their child is guilty. Even the most notorious serial killers often had mothers who stood by them and refused to believe they did the things they were accused of.

Mary Bell didn't like talking about her family to psychiatrists while she was in custody. They struggled to get much information out of her. The authorities knew though that her house was dirty and barely furnished and that her mother was a prostitute who spent more time in Glasgow than Newcastle. Her father was a jailbird and petty criminal. The case of Mary Bell touches on the debate of nature v nurture. The nature versus nurture debate is a longstanding discussion in psychology and behavioural science centred around the relative contributions of genetics (nature) and environmental factors (nurture) to human development, personality, and behaviour. Proponents of the nature side argue that genetic inheritance plays a crucial role in shaping an individual's characteristics, such as intelligence, temperament, and susceptibility to certain diseases. This perspective is often supported by studies in fields like genetics and neurobiology, which illustrate how specific genes can influence traits and behaviour.

The nurture camp posits that environmental influences, such as upbringing, culture, education, and life experiences, significantly impact behaviour and personality development. This view emphasises the malleability of human beings and how experiences in early childhood, social interactions, and learned behaviour can shape an individual over time. Modern research increasingly suggests that the interplay between nature and nurture is complex, with many traits influenced by a dynamic interaction between an individual's genetic makeup and their environment. For instance, a person may have a genetic predisposition for a particular ability or behaviour, but whether that trait fully develops can depend significantly on external factors like educational opportunities, social support, and cultural context. Thus, the essence of human behaviour and development can often be better understood by acknowledging both the innate biological factors and the rich tapestry of experiences that shape each individual's life.

Mary Bell later admitted that being a liar had become second nature to her by now. Most of what she told the police was lies and the psychiatrists didn't fare much better. This is why her later claims of childhood sexual assault were not believed by everyone. No one doubted that Mary Bell had a difficult and abusive childhood, she had the hospital visits to prove that, but her claims of being forced into prostitution by her mother are not easy to verify. No one really knew if Mary Bell ever told the truth about anything. One problem with the sexual abuse allegations is that Mary's aunts took an interest in her life and looked out for her as best they could. If they had learned that Betty Bell was allowing men to sexually abuse Mary they surely would have acted to protect their niece. If she really was allowing Mary to be sexually abused, Betty would have had to keep this hidden from Billy, her sisters, and her other children. It's hard to see how this could have been done in that cramped house perched on a claustrophobic street where everyone knew everyone and there were few secrets. Betty did not going around broadcasting she was a prostitute but everyone in the area knew she was a 'lady of the night'.

Betty Bell was now required to be a more responsible and active mother than she had been in the past. She attended interviews with Mary and a solicitor, often with Billy in attendance. Mary Bell heard the solicitor mention that Norma that was considered the more immature of the two defendants. Mary was sharp enough to realise that being considered more intelligent than Norma might be more of a curse than a blessing when it came to assigning blame for what had happened. Although she gained a reputation for being a very sharp and intelligent child, Mary had already shot herself in the foot by bringing up the scissors in police interviews and she would also get herself into a muddle in court when she seemed to try to adjust her evidence in accordance with what was happening in the trial. As a result of this Mary's court evidence eventually began to contradict her police statements and interviews. Mary's attempts to improvise in court did not do her much good in the end.

Retrospectives of the Mary Bell case sometimes tend to portray her as a spooky child who creeped out the people who looked after her in custody. She is alleged to have told police officers that she liked hurting little things that couldn't fight back. It seems unlikely that Mary Bell was stupid enough to do this because that would have been an admission of guilt. Mary Bell had no intention of confessing to these crimes or accepting the fate which was apparently in store once this case was progressed to a court. She was determined to keep up the pretence that she had nothing to do with these deaths. The biggest difference between Mary and Norma in custody is that Mary was confident around adults while Norma was shy. Norma's resting face often made her looked bewildered. Norma seemed more vulnerable and confused than Mary to the adults who who encountered them before the trial. This was an advantage to Norma in court (albeit an advantage that she was oblivious to).

Another advantage Norma had is that her police statement seemed more credible and plausible than the one supplied by Mary Bell. Mary Bell's statement was full of improbable little tangents, like her claim that after murdering Brian Howe, a crazed foaming at the mouth Norma had then tried to strangle Brian Howe's dog. These sorts of details sounded like an eleven year-old making something up because that's exactly what they were. In her police statement, Mary depicted Norma as a dangerous violent maniac who was planning to run away from home. The adults who looked after Norma in custody saw no evidence of this dangerous maniac. They also saw no evidence for why Norma would run away from home seeing as she had two loving parents who were doing a great job of supporting her in the run up to the trial. What they didn't know was that Norma HAD run away from home more than once - going missing for two days on one occasion. Norma, like her friend Mary Bell, was not the easiest person to comprehend.

KILLER KIDS

There have been very few cases in Britain since 1968 where a killer was as young as Mary Bell or younger still. This is really what gives the Mary Bell story its power and horrible fascination. There have though been a number of horrendous cases where killers were of a similar age to Mary Bell. Sharon Carr was born in Belize and moved to Surry with her family when she was about five. Carr would become Britain's youngest female murderer (Mary Bell was younger than Carr when she killed but Mary Bell was convicted for manslaughter) in 1992 when she stabbed to death 18 year-old Katie Rackliff in Camberley. Katie Rackliff was a hairdresser who was walking home from a nightclub. Carr picked her out at random and stabbed Rackliff over 30 times. It was a sickening attack with the victim stabbed, among other places, in the private parts and backside. The victim also had knife wounds to the heart and ribs. Sharon Carr was somewhat like a much younger version of Joanna Dennehy.

Sharon Carr was just twelve years-old when she committed this dreadful murder. She was with two boys at the time. Some accounts of this case say that Katie Rackliff had argued with her boyfriend that night and accepted a lift from the boys and that it was Carr who lured her into the car. However, the boys had nothing to do with the murder and were much later eliminated from police inquiries. They were certainly not present during the murder and had no idea that Carr planned to kill Katie. Because of the ferocity of the attack and the mutilation of the sexual organs the police assumed that the killer was an adult male serial killer and that this was a sexually motivated crime. Never in a million years could they have guessed that the depraved killer in this case was a twelve year-old girl.

The severity of the wounds had indicated that only someone with adult strength could have done this but that obviously wasn't the case. For this reason Sharon Carr seemed to get away with the crime - for a time at least. It beggared belief that a girl of twelve could have the savagery and heartlessness to do something like this. Carr's home life, you probably won't be surprised to hear, was no bed of roses. She came from what you might call a broken home and her family had little money. Carr was a deeply disturbed child with serious mental health problems. There was soon more evidence for this two years later when Carr stabbed a fellow pupil at Collingwood College Comprehensive School. The pupil was stabbed in the lung and barely survived. The attack was random and took place in the toilets. Carr was taken into custody and sent to a medical assessment centre - where she tried to throttle two members of staff. It would be something of an understatement to say that Sharon Carr was not the full shilling. She was violent and highly dangerous but thankfully now out of society.

Carr was eventually sent to HM Prison Bullwood Hall in Essex. This facility was closed in 2013 but at the time it was a prison for women and young offenders. Bullwood Prison had a population of about 184 women prisoners and had workshops, training and education facilities. At this time the authorities still had no idea that Carr had murdered Katie Rackliff. That crime was still unsolved. It was only during her time in prison that Sharon Carr's murder of Katie Rackliff came to light. Carr was apparently overheard boasting about this murder to family and friends and even to prison staff. That was certainly a strange thing to boast about. Carr's mental capacity was illustrated by the fact that she was basically shooting her own foot off by talking of this murder. It could be that she just didn't care or simply didn't have the mental capacity to realise what she was doing. While some boasts of those in prison turn out to be delusions or even hot air the authorities had a duty to investigate the possibility that Carr was telling the truth.

The police managed to seize Carr's diaries and found entries where Carr wrote about Rackliff's murder and talked about her desire to kill. "I was born to be a murderer. Killing for me is a mass turn-on and it just makes me so high I never want to come down. Every night I see the Devil in my dreams - sometimes even in my mirror, but I realise it was just me." Sharon Carr confessed all to the police and the identity of Katie Rackliff's killer was finally solved. Nothing would ever bring Katie back but at least her family now had a sense of closure and justice. Sharon Carr was most likely never going to get out of prison now. It was a place she was sadly always destined to end up from a preposterously young age. The police and medical experts who spoke to Carr found her highly disturbing. She had no remorse and no compassion or sense of guilt. She was simply a deeply sick and troubled person. Sharon Carr was the most dangerous type of killer imaginable because she killed at random with no motive. Had she not been taken into custody for the school attack there is no doubt that she would eventually have killed again. The girl she attacked at school was very fortunate to survive what was clearly an attempted murder.

Carr was found guilty of murder at her trial and given a minimum sentence of 14 years. She eventually ended up at Broadmoor Hospital after being sectioned under the Mental Health Act. Carr was later transferred to HM Prison Low Newton. She has lately been held in HMP Bronzefield in south-west London. Carr has continued to attack staff and other inmates while incarcerated. She is now 42 years-old but the chances of her ever being released are slim to say the least - despite her appeals. Would you want to live next door to Sharon Carr? No, me neither. Carr tends to be known as The Devil's Daughter in true crime. She was one of the most dangerous teenagers in British criminal history. Experts judged Carr to be suffering from schizoaffective disorder. Schizoaffective disorder is a condition where symptoms of both psychotic and mood disorders are present together during one episode or within a two week period of each other. This condition can cause hallucinations, delusions, depressions, and mania. Sharon Carr will only be eligible for parole if she isn't sectioned. Even if she isn't sectioned her chances of parole are slim. As such she is likely to be a very old woman by the time anyone would seriously consider releasing her.

In April 2016, a dreadful and harrowing double murder took place in Spalding, Lincolnshire. The victims were a mother named Elizabeth Edwards and her thirteen year-old daughter Katie. The mastermind of the murders was the other daughter Kim Edwards. She had not acted alone in these evil murders because her boyfriend Lucas Markham had been more than willing to kill these family members for her. It was shocking enough that someone would murder their mother and sister but most shocking of all was the fact that Kim Edwards and Lucas Markham were only fourteen years-old at the time. Kim Edwards and Lucas Markham quickly developed an intense bond when they met. They both had suicidal thoughts and clearly found a kindred spirit in one another. Both felt like outcasts in the world until they found one another. From that point on it was them against the world. Or, to be more precise, them against the other members of Kim's family. Kim Edwards and Lucas Markham fell further and further into their own dark fantasy world. Experts who have studied this case believe that these murders would not have happened if Kim Edwards and Lucas Markham had never met. You could say then that these two troubled teens truly brought out the worst in one another.

There was another sister in the family named Mary but she was older and (thankfully for her) lived in Derby. Mary said that she deduced fairly quickly that Lucas Markham was bad news but Kim would not hear a bad word said about him. The more that people said Markham was no good, well, the more this just made Kim want to be with him. Markham was Kim's first boyfriend and the first person her own age she'd ever felt a connection with. Kim Edwards had become increasingly embittered because she believed her mother loved her younger sister Katie more than her. This was a figment of her self-centred imagination. Elizabeth loved all her daughters equally. It seems that Kim became jealous of Katie and so began to hate her mother. Kim's mother also tried to stop her from seeing Markham and this increased the tension between mother and daughter. It got to a point where Markham was banned from coming in the house so the two teen lovers had to have secret meetings. The illicit and forbidden nature of their relationship only served to make their bond stronger. They felt like everyone was against them.

Kim's father had left when she was two years-old. Elizabeth Edwards did not have a happy marriage and apparently had to use a women's refuge to escape from violence at home. As such, she had brought the girls up as a single-parent. Kim had clearly struggled to cope with having a younger sibling. She seemed to resent not being the centre of attention anymore when Katie was born. Kim Edwards was highly disturbed and dangerous. Tragically, her boyfriend was no less disturbed and was more than happy to participate in her deadly plans. When it comes to teen criminals these two awful kids were straight out of central casting. Kim Edwards had huge blank dark eyes and looked completely crazy. There was a weird detachment to her photographs as if she wasn't actually there in spirit. Her boyfriend Lucas Markham also looked like a complete psychopath. He resembled the missing link in his police mugshot and his narrow beady eyes made him seem spinster and angry. Even in photos where Markham is smiling he looks like he's about to kill someone. It's a great tragedy that these two ever met in the first place.

The tension between Kim and her mother had a long history. Elizabeth shopped herself to social services in 2008 when she hit Kim during a row at home. The girls were temporarily taken into care as a consequence. Elizabeth Edwards believed that she was never able to repair her relationship with Kim after this. She always suspected that Kim was planning to run away from home. In 2013, Kim told social workers that her mother had tried to strangle her but this claim was found to have no credibility. Kim had actually run away with Markham in 2015 - though the pair were quickly found. They had been sleeping rough in the woods. This incident highlighted how these two teens were detached from reality. You can't run away from your life and the real world at the age of 14 by living in the woods. The more estranged that Kim became from her family the closer she got to Markham. The great tragedy of this case is that it was all in Kim's imagination. Her mother loved her no less than her other daughters and always did her best.

In fact, only days before she was murdered Elizabeth Edwards sent affectionate messages to Kim on Facebook. It's not as if Elizabeth was Miss Murdstone from David Copperfield. Everyone who knew Elizabeth - aside from Kim - liked her. Things continued on a troubled path for Kim Edwards and Lucas Markham in 2015. She took an overdose of pills and Markham was expelled from school. Markham was unremarkable in school. No one really noticed him much. Kim felt the same so when they found one another their bond was unusually strong - even for teenagers. Lucas Markham was taken into foster care at the age of four and then lived with an aunt. His mother died of cancer when he was very young. Those who knew Markham at school said he could be very quiet but then suddenly snap and be volatile and angry. The first time that Kim Edwards ever saw Markham was when he angrily threw a chair in the classroom. This act of rebellion clearly made an impression on her.

Kim was later judged to be suffering from adjustment disorder. An adjustment disorder is an emotional or behavioural reaction to a stressful event or change in a person's life. Her mental problems felt far more complex than that though. Everything in her life was blown out of all proportion in her mind. By now Kim had absurdly and tragically come to the conclusion that the solution to all her problems was to kill her mother. She had also decided that her sister Katie must die too. Kim felt that with her mother out of the way she would no longer have anyone to prevent her from seeing Markham. The rather obvious flaw in this plan is that she was highly unlikely to ever see Markham again if they murdered her mother together. They were hardly likely to be put in the same prison cell. Such details are beyond the grasp of mentally troubled teenage killers though. These basic facts simply don't seem to occur to them.

These evil young lovers actually had two aborted attempts to kill Elizabeth and Katie. Their plan was for Kim Edwards to wait until her mother and sister had gone to sleep and then open a window for Markham to get into the house and kill them. Two times though Kim fell asleep before she was supposed to let Markham in. The house was located in an ordinary suburban street. It isn't as if Lucas Markham was going to have much cover or any places to hide as he waited outside. These two teenagers had long since fallen down the rabbit hole of fantasy and delusion. Any grasp they once had on reality was almost non-existent. The third attempt to go through with the plan was - tragically - more successful. Kim did not fall asleep on this night. She waited until her mother and sister had gone to sleep and then opened the window to let the lurking Markham into the house. Markham had brought a bag of kitchen knives with him. He then went into the bedroom and smothered Elizabeth Edwards with a pillow while he stabbed her in the throat.

Markham was instructed by Kim to target the voice box with his knife so that Elizabeth couldn't make any noise. It is impossible really to comprehend how evil and heartless these two kids were. Once Elizabeth Edwards was dead, Markham killed Katie in the same fashion - by smothering her and stabbing her in the neck. Kim was supposed to stab Katie herself but she couldn't go through with it. Not that she gains any credit for this. She'd still wanted her sister to die. Kim Edwards later said that the deaths were quick but they were most assuredly not. Elizabeth and Katie did not die instantly and suffered greatly at the hands of this disturbed teenage lunatic. When the murders were complete, Kim Edwards and Lucas Markham had a bath to wash the blood off and then had sex. They then got themselves some ice-cream and cakes and watched the vampire film series Twilight. This detail in the case is why they are often referred to as The Twilight Killers in true crime circles. They did all of these things with the blood drenched bodies of Elizabeth and Katie only a room or two away.

Where these two kids truly evil or were they simply insane? Well, maybe it was a bit of both. Their sense of detachment was astonishing. They had just stabbed Kim's kid sister and mother to death but now settled down to watch films without a care in the world. Kim Edwards and Markham made no attempt to flee or hide their crimes. They simply stayed in the house and acted as if nothing had happened. A relative of the family actually knocked on the door at one point but they simply hid and didn't answer. In the end though the two kids were reported missing because they hadn't turned up at school. Around this time Elizabeth had been in a relationship with a man named Graham Green. Green was away a lot because he worked on a ship at sea. He contacted the police though when he couldn't get in contact with Elizabeth. The police turned up at the house and forced their way in. The police officer who entered the house first asked the two kids where Mrs Edwards was. Lucas Markham told him to go upstairs and see for himself.

When the police saw the bodies for themselves they rather

taken aback as you might imagine. It was not just that these two kids had killed but also the way they were acting. Kim Edwards and Lucas Markham simply didn't care. They were happy and relieved. They seemed to think they had done a good thing by killing Elizabeth and Katie. Markham later told the police - "She (Edwards) always hated her mum and I said 'I wish I could kill her' and she said 'yeah', and thought I was joking - but I was being serious. Then she realised I was being serious, so she started being serious." When he was asked why they had killed Katie, Markham said it was because she would have called the police. That was cold and illogical logic in its purest form. Did this idiot really think they were going to get away with these murders? Did they kill Katie merely to buy themselves enough time to enjoy the house alone for a few days? Kim Edwards seemed to believe she had done her mother and sister a favour by killing them. She said they wouldn't have to suffer any more heartbreak in life. Kim Edwards was what you might call an egocentric psychopath. She was wicked beyond words.

The details of this case were absolutely horrific. The two teen killers were not even named in the press at first - such was the horrendous nature of the case. Neither displayed any remorse or emotion in their police interviews. Both talked about the murders in a bland matter of fact way as if it had all been no big deal. Kim Edwards said that she still felt content about the deaths and had no regrets. Kim Edwards tried to plead guilty of manslaughter on the grounds of diminished responsibility but experts judged that there was nothing wrong with her. Markham also tried the same plea but got short shrift too. The full weight of the law was going to come down hard on these two teenagers. Though they once had an unbreakable bond which drove them to murder it is interesting how they began to drift apart in custody. Markham refused to speak at first but then learned that Kim was openly talking to the police. He was annoyed when he heard about this.

Kim was said to have felt betrayed too when Markham changed his plea to murder from manslaughter. Kim was also annoyed when Markham's lawyer tried to portray her as the mastermind and argue that Markham was some gullible dupe who had been manipulated. The truth is they were both as bad as each other. Kim Edwards and Markham were fifteen when they were sentenced to a minimum of 20 years at Nottingham Crown Court. They were Britain's youngest double murderers. The court heard that Markham had been left with scratch marks after killing Elizabeth Edwards because she had struggled and fought for some minutes before she was killed. She did this as a knife was being plunged into her neck.

The murder of innocent 13 year-old Katie was beyond evil. What had she ever done to anyone? The judge called the murders "a terrible crime which has few parallels in modern criminal history." The court heard how Kim Edwards and Markham had then spent two days in the house watching movies while the bodies of the victims lay upstairs. Mary Edwards, the other sister, later said to to the newspapers - "I knew my sister was unhinged, I just didn't think she was that unhinged." Mary had gone to the trial but was disgusted to see that her sister displayed no remorse - not even for the murder of Katie. Mary was especially sickened that Kim smirked at her in court.

This was a harrowing case to have to attend. The jury were disgusted by what they heard and one member of the gallery started shouting at Kim Edwards and Markham at one point when the court was told that they'd eaten ice-cream and watched a film after the murders. It also transpired in court that this diabolical duo had planned the murders in a local McDonald's. Friends of Elizabeth Edwards were appalled and angered by this murder. They had found her to be a kind and friendly person. It's safe to say that Kim Edwards and Lucas

Markham had zero sympathy. This was one of those cases where most people just wanted the authorities to lock them up and throw the key away. Their sentences were reduced to 17 and a half years on appeal - meaning they would be eligible for release in their thirties. Whether or not this will happen remains to be seen.

If they are released they are unlikely to have much of a life. They will have to have new identities and live in fear of the media and public finding out who they really are. Their employment prospects will be minimal too. Kim Edwards and Lucas Markham, if they are ever released, will also be banned from having any contact. When one reads about this case and looks at the smiling photos of poor Katie Edwards you can't hoping that Kim Edwards and Lucas Markham spend a lot more time in prison than their sentences might indicate. One person who definitely never wants Kim released is Graham Green. When this dreadful case was finally over he compared Kim to Myra Hindley. In his view Kim Edwards is one of the most evil females in British true crime history.

On 28 April 2014, 61 year-old language teacher Ann Maguire, as usual, went to work at Corpus Christi Catholic College in Halton Moor, Leeds, Yorkshire. Ann Maguire was a highly valued and much respected teacher who loved her job. Ann had plans to retire soon and was looking forward to spending more time at home. A happy retirement would be a deserved reward for her many dedicated years working in education. Fate can be cruel and random though and the plans of Ann Maguire would sadly not come to pass. She had no idea that this fateful day at school was to be the last day of her life. The Spanish class she taught that day included a 15 year-old boy named William "Will" Cornick. Ann Maguire had been teaching Cornick since he was about eleven so they knew each other well. Cornick had a festering dislike of Ann Maguire which had now become an all consuming obsession. He had commented to friends that he would like to murder her and even joked on Facebook that he would give £10 to anyone who killed Ann Maguire. This was all taken with a pinch of salt by his friends. They presumed he was just joking.

Two months previously, Cornick had said to a friend on Facebook of Ann Maguire - "...the one absolute f****** bitch that deserves more than death more than pain torture and more than anything that we can understand." Cornick would joke to friends about how great it would be if Ann Maguire got hit by a train or taken out by a sniper. Developing a dislike for a teacher is nothing new for kids. We all probably had a few teachers at school we didn't care for too much. In the case of Cornick though this was no laughing matter. His intense dislike of Ann Maguire would unfathomably boil over into tragedy and violence. On the fateful day in question Cornick had secretly brought a kitchen knife to school with him. He'd also packed a smaller knife. It later transpired that he'd shown the larger knife to some other kids at school. They had no idea that he actually planned to use it for anything. They thought he was just trying to act tough.

The Spanish lesson took place after the morning break. Cornick had no criminal record and a comfortable and stable family background. He lived with his mother (who worked in human resources) in a pleasant enough house. His parents were divorced but he saw his father, who worked for the local council, often. There was nothing obvious in Cornick's past or present to indicate that he was highly dangerous or patently disturbed. A week earlier Cornick had seemed happy enough while attending his grandmother's birthday party. He had never got into any major trouble at school and was generally regarded to be a good pupil and a decent kid. Those who knew Cornick said he was polite and one of the last people you'd ever expect to get into serious trouble. Appearances can obviously be deceptive though. No one could possibly have known of the anger and dark thoughts now swirling around in the troubled mind of Will Cornick. Cornick's dislike for Ann

Maguire was about to change his life forever and shatter the lives of her family and relatives.

Friction between them seemed to come to a head when Ann Maguire banned Cornick from a school trip for not doing his Spanish homework. Cornick ignored her and attended the trip anyway but he did not take this punishment lightly. When he attended a parents meeting at school with his mum and dad, Cornick had created a scene by refusing to meet or talk with Ann Maguire. He could literally not even stand being in the same room as her. His dislike of Ann Maguire was beginning to dominate his life. He could barely think of anything else. Despite his age, the gangling Cornick was already 6'2 in height. Ann Maguire was only 5'2. His savage attack on her was therefore justifiably regarded to be cowardly. At the time of the murder, Cornick had long ridiculous teenage hair which made him look rather like Harry Enfield's comedy television character Kevin the Teenager. His main feature was his blank dark eyes. This was a boy now with little in the way of natural human emotion - besides anger.

Cornick had been diagnosed with diabetes - which had apparently put a spanner in his dream of joining the army. This was hardly a justification for murder but it seemed to effect some alarming mood changes in Cornick. Kids at school had noticed a gallows humour darkness about him which hadn't been apparent before. All that stuff about wanting Ann Maguire to die was a case in point. In addition to a kitchen knife, Cornick had taken a bottle of Scotch to school with him that day. The alcohol was for the celebration he planned after murdering Ann Maguire. This was no random spur of the moment act. Cornick had carefully planned this murder. He had been thinking about it for a long time.

After about half an hour of the Spanish lesson Ann was teaching that morning, Cornick came in and - to the horror and astonishment of all who were there - began to stab Ann

Maguire with a kitchen knife. Ann Maguire was leaning over a desk helping another pupil with something when Cornick attacked her from behind. The diminutive and distracted teacher was taken by complete surprise by this sadistic 6'2 coward.

Ann, now obviously in complete shock, was stabbed several times in the back and neck by the crazed Will Cornick. It was a truly horrific scene. Another teacher heard the screams and rushed to see what was happening. This teacher was named Susan Francis. By now Ann Maguire had staggered out into a corridor but Cornick had followed her to continue his harrowing and tragic attack. Even as Ann fled he continued to stab her, Susan Francis bravely managed to separate Ann Maguire from Cornick and get Ann into an empty classroom. As she did this she get her foot on the door to stop Cornick getting in. Francis later said of Cornick - "I just remember his face having no emotion on it, none at all. It was like a mask on his face, no emotion." Susan Francis then screamed at a nearby male teacher to come and help. Ann Maguire knew she was dying. She told Francis as much as the teacher held her. Though paramedics arrived and did their best to save Ann Maguire it was too late. She had been stabbed in a jugular vein and died of her injuries. She lost consciousness in the ambulance on the way to to hospital and never woke up again.

Craig Sagar, one of the paramedics that day, said the injuries to Ann Maguire were the worst he'd ever seen. Cornick had used such force that the knife had gone from 'front to back' in the victim. After the attack on Ann Maguire, Cornick simply sat down again and commented "good times" to the other pupils. The fact that he had just stabbed a teacher in the neck several times wasn't something that bothered him in the slightest. Cornick was then taken into the school lobby by two teachers to await the police. The first police officer to arrive was, like everyone else, struck by how calm Cornick was. Cornick was acting as if nothing had happened. He asked the police officer for some ice for his hand (never mind poor Ann Maguire, Cornick was only concerned about his hand hurting) and then even inquired what the officer's favourite film was. When he was placed in custody, Cornick told the police that everything was "fine and dandy" now.

When he was arrested and evaluated, Cornick told a psychiatrist - "I wanted to get caught. That's why I did it in school. I wanted to be in jail. I wasn't in shock, I was happy. I had a sense of pride. I still do. I know it's uncivilised but I know it's incredibly instinctual and human. Past generations of life, killing is a route of survival. It's kill or be killed. I did not have a choice. It was kill her or suicide. I know the victim's family will be upset but I don't care. I couldn't give a s***" At the trial, Cornick pleaded guilty. The family of Ann Maguire felt the whole case was handled very shabbily and they were annoyed that there wasn't initially a proper inquest which interviewed fellow pupils of Cornick. An inquest, which the authorities tried to block, was eventually held and judged that Ann Maguire's life could have been saved because warning signs about Cornick were apparent. The prosecution's leading psychiatric expert said that Cornick had a "gross lack of empathy for his victim and a degree of callousness rarely seen in clinical practice."

Experts judged that Cornick suffered from adjustment disorder. Adjustment disorder is a condition in which a person displays an exaggerated response to a stressful or difficult event. Cornick's 'stressful' event was that he didn't get on very well with one of his teachers. This is something we've all experienced but we don't then stab the teacher in question to death as a consequence. Cornick was, to state the obvious, a deeply troubled and highly dangerous kid. Will Cornick was sentenced to a minimum of 20 years and told by the judge that even when that time had elapsed he might never be released. It will be a highly controversial decision indeed if Will Cornick is ever released in the future. He appealed the sentence but this appeal was unsuccessful. Sometimes with very young criminals and even killers it is possible to have some degree of sympathy for them in the case of a stern sentence and suggest that rehabilitation could be possible. It was very difficult though to have this attitude with Will Cornick. There can be few people who didn't believe he deserved to be locked up for decades.

Cornick showed no remorse for his crime and generally didn't seem to care less that he had brutally taken the life of a beloved wife, mother, and teacher. There was a vague attempt by Cornick's legal team to say that 'voices' had made him commit the murder but this felt like a rather desperate attempt to make it seem like he hadn't been of sound mind and didn't know what he was doing. Cornick clearly knew what he was doing. There was even evidence that he had planned to kill Ann Maguire four days earlier than he actually did. Pupils said that Cornick had even told them he planned to kill other teachers - including one who was pregnant. Cornick was very intelligent for his age and had even taken some of his GCSEs early. Those who knew him at school said he didn't really stand out much and wasn't someone you tended to notice. It later transpired that Cornick's girlfriend had dumped him shortly before the murder. This added another layer of instability to Cornick's already troubled state of mind. The girl in question later left the school because the shame of being briefly associated with the now notorious Cornick was too much.

A kid at the school later told the media that he wished he'd reported seeing Cornick with a knife to teachers and wonders if this tragedy could have been averted. While the fact that Cornick had brought knives to school should have been reported by the kids who saw them the trouble is, as we have noted, that no one suspected that Cornick was actually planning to use one of them. This case was obviously rough on Cornick's parents. They got death threats on social media after Cornick's identity was revealed in the newspapers. The parents of Will Cornick said they were at a loss to explain how their son turned out like this. He didn't come from a broken home and he wasn't neglected or abused. Cornick's father later told the media that his son was sorry for what he had done and was trying to get better and be a good person. Even if that was true (and that was a big IF given what the despicable Cornick had done and how he acted afterwards) it was all a bit late now and scant solace for Ann Maguire's family.

On the 25th of April 2011 there was a fire in a house located in a fairly comfortable and sedate area of Nottingham. Forty-seven year-old Jacqueline Bartlam did not escape from the house and perished. However, her fourteen year-old son Daniel Bartlam somehow managed to get himself, his younger brother, and the family dog out of the house to safety. At first glance it appeared that Daniel had been something of a hero in his actions that tragic night. Alas, this wasn't the case at all. This strange affair was about to take a plunge into the bizarre. Daniel told the police that an intruder had entered the house that night and then started a fire. He said he'd managed to escape with his younger brother but his mother hadn't been so lucky. Daniel was basically portraying himself as a hero that night. To listen to his story he'd been a plucky brave kid battling the flames and smoke to save his little brother.

It didn't take long for Daniel Bartlam's story to come crashing down around his young ears. The police forensics team managed to retrieve Jacqueline Bartlam's body from the house before it had been too badly damaged by the fire. She hadn't burned to death or suffocated in the smoke. She had been bludgeoned to death with a claw hammer. Jacqueline was already dead before the fire even started. The police also managed to get hold of Daniel Bartlam's computer - which had been spared the flames - and examined the contents. The computer revealed that Daniel was obsessed with a villain in the soap opera Coronation Street called John Stape. In the show Stape had killed a character and tried to mask his handiwork. Daniel was clearly something of a soap opera buff because the police found that he'd saved clips of various murderous soap opera villains going about their grisly (if sanitised) mainstream early evening business. This case was now quickly falling into place. There was no intruder as Daniel had claimed. As unlikely as it might have seemed at first glance it was now apparent that this fourteen year-old kid was now the prime suspect in the frightful murder of his mother.

There is only one problem with someone using soap opera villains as the basis for a real crime. Soap operas are fictitious. They are the work of writers trying to entertain people. Daniel seemed bafflingly and naively unaware of this inescapable fact. Daniel Bartlam also had a fondness for writing macabre stories on his computer - in some of them even writing fantasies about killing his mother. You didn't need to be Jessica Fletcher by now to deduce that young Daniel Bartlam had lied through his teeth about what happened the night his mother died. Someone who definitely knew that Daniel was lying was Jacqueline's partner Simon Matters - who was essentially Daniel's step-father. Simon Matters had never liked Daniel much and always found him to be a disturbing and weird kid. Matters had even seen some of the fiction Daniel had written about killing his mother. When he heard about the fire and Jacqueline's death, Simon Matters had no doubt at all that Daniel Bartlam had been responsible.

It transpired that Daniel Bartlam had sneaked into his mother's room at night and struck her several times with a claw hammer until she was dead. This was a very violent murder because he struck his mother in the head with the hammer. He had then wrapped her body in newspaper and set fire to it. Daniel is believed to have used some petrol for this. He then dropped another hammer by the body to make it look as if an intruder had dropped this weapon. As for the actual hammer he used, he cleaned this with cleaning products and then hid it in the shed. Daniel then got his brother and dog out of the house. When neighbours came out into the street to see what was happening, Daniel told them about the 'intruder' to plant the seed of his fictitious cover story. He thought he had committed the perfect murder but fourteen year-olds tend not to be criminal masterminds and Daniel Bartlam's grisly ruse soon fell apart under scrutiny from the police and the evidence found in the house.

The intruder theory never had any credibility at all because who would randomly break into a house in an ordinary Nottingham street to bludgeon a middle-aged mother of two to death and set fire to the home? That didn't really fit the MO of your average killer and if it wasn't random why on earth would anyone target Jacqueline Bartlam? Daniel Bartlam was previously at a private school - although he'd been moved to a state school in the end when the fees became too much for his mother to cope with. He had undergone counselling sessions for anger issues and his claim that he heard voices in his head. Those that dealt with him though after he was arrested could find nothing obviously wrong with him. Daniel Bartlam, once his murder had been exposed, told the police that he had killed his mother in an act of self-defence because she was abusive. This would be the defence that his legal team offered in court. This claim did not fly very far at all when examined and put to the test. Simon Matters told the authorities that it was the other way around. He said Daniel was abusive. Matters told the police that he'd often had to step in to protect Jacqueline from her son.

The trial established that Daniel had not been telling the truth about the abuse. If anything his mother had been too soft with him. Daniel Bartlam was said to be a fairly normal kid to those that knew him. He liked Doctor Who and Star Wars and seemed reasonably intelligent. In reality though he was clearly troubled. There was once an incident at school where Daniel became convinced that his tie was sentient and was trying to kill him. Simon Matters said that Daniel would defecate in his own bedroom and had a habit of stealing his mother's underwear. Matters had always worried that Daniel might do something really bad one day. As ever in these cases, much was made in the media of the fact that Daniel apparently enjoyed horror movies and FPS video games. Where one to take this dubious catch all link between pop culture and crime literally then presumably Coronation Street would have to be banned too given its connection to this case!

At his trial, Daniel Bartlam pleaded not-guilty. This was clearly a futile gesture. "Unfortunately for you," said the judge to Daniel, "it was more difficult to destroy a body than you thought and the pathologist, who examined your mother's body, was able to say with certainty that the attack had been with a claw hammer, rather than the lump hammer you left in the room." Daniel was given life with a minimum of 16 years. He is eligible for parole in 2027 and it seems more than likely that he might be released one day. One person who finds this prospect rather appalling is Simon Matters. He doesn't believe that Daniel can be rehabilitated and thinks it's for the best if his former step-son is locked up for good. Time will tell if Daniel Bartlam, now forever destined to be known as The Coronation Street Killer in true crime, will ever see the light of day again.

MARY v NORMA

Mary Bell was housed at Fernwood Remand Home in Newcastle for the trial. This was where the police had once taken Norma to make it easier to question her in private. The streets of Scotswood must have seemed a little quieter and a little less dangerous for other children without Mary and

Norma wandering around anymore. The trial of Mary Bell and Norma Joyce Bell began at the Newcastle Assizes Moot Hall on December the 5th 1968. The trial lasted just nine days in the end. Mr Justice Cusack was selected as the judge. Sir Ralph Vincent Cusack had been a judge for about four years. He made his name successfully defending two journalists in the famous 1962 Vassall Tribunal. The Vassall Tribunal, also known as the Vassall Inquiry, was established in response to the Vassall Affair, a scandal involving the British civil servant and spy, John Vassall. Vassall was a clerk in the Ministry of War who was arrested in 1962 after being found guilty of espionage. He had been passing sensitive information to the Soviet Union in exchange for money, which he later used to fund a lavish lifestyle.

The tribunal was set up to investigate the circumstances surrounding Vassall's espionage activities, the failures of the security services, and the broader implications for British national security. It aimed to review how Vassall managed to infiltrate sensitive government areas and the extent of the damage caused by his actions. The inquiry revealed significant shortcomings in the British intelligence and security systems at the time, particularly concerning the screening of personnel in critical positions and the handling of potential security threats. The revelations from the tribunal raised serious questions about the effectiveness and robustness of Britain's Cold War espionage protocols. The Vassall Affair and the subsequent tribunal had notable repercussions, including calls for reforms in security practices within government departments, and it highlighted the risks posed by individuals in sensitive positions who could be compromised. Mr Justice Cusack was highly respected and handled the trial of Mary and Norma in a very calm and almost gentle way. He was very conscious of the fact that the defendants were children and adjusted the usual style of a court trial in accordance with that.

Mary was defended by Harvey Robson QC; Norma by R. P. Smith QC. Rudolph Lyons QC was the chief prosecutor. The barristers for Mary and Norma were paid by legal aid. Mary's barrister was much older than Norma's barrister. Mary and Norma were both charged with the murders of Martin Brown and Brian Howe and both pleaded not-guilty. The trial was moved to the smaller courtroom two because it was felt a bigger court would be too overwhelming for the two girls. Mary and Norma also didn't have to sit in the dock. They were allowed to sit at tables in the centre of the court. There were some police officers guarding them but this seemed more like a legal formality to be adhered to rather than a necessity. It wasn't as if two young girls were going to overpower the security guard and make a dash for freedom.

Though they were obviously separated, Mary and Norma made eye contact at the start of the trial and smiled at one another but when they started giving evidence the last flames of the bond between these two girls soon went out. They would both complain out loud when the other said something in court they didn't like. Norma in particular was audibly annoyed whenever she was cast as the killer by Mary in court. In the end the judge had to warn the two girls to stay quiet when someone else was giving evidence. The defendants' right to anonymity was waived by the judge on the first day of the trial. This meant the identities and ages of the two girls on trial for murder could be fully released and reported on. The public and press were shocked when they saw the ages and gender of the two defendants but the case did not get anywhere near the coverage it might today. There were surprisingly few members of the press in attendance at the start of the trial though more did turn up when the trial was more advanced and a verdict got closer.

The families of Mary and Norma were all in court to support them. Mary had her mother, Billy Bell, her grandmother (who was Betty's mother) and aunts. Billy Bell's sister Audrey and her husband Peter were also in court as was the mother of John Best, the cousin who Mary Bell had injured. John Best's mother turned up to lend support to Mary Bell - oblivious to Mary's ill treatment of her son. Norma had her parents and even some of her siblings. Neither of the mothers of Martin Brown and Brian Howe attended the trial. Martin's mother June could not face hearing about his death all over again while Brian's mother Eileen was too ill to attend. The question of whether two people as young as Mary Bell and Norma should have been on trial in a real court was a complex one and not easy to answer. In his summing up near the end of the trial, Mr Justice Cusack alluded to this himself when he said the law states that anyone over the age of ten can be placed on trial for serious crimes. Mr Justice Cusack said that the law can't be applied as we might like to 'rewrite' it in our 'heart'. In a reasonably subtle way, this was Cusack expressing his own doubts that the formality of an Assize Court was really the best place for these two girls to be processed.

The trial began with a lengthy opening speech by Rudolph Lyons QC for the prosecution. Mr Lyons contended that both girls were equally culpable for the murders and had committed these crimes purely for their own amusement. Mr Lyons talked about the similarities in the circumstances of the deaths of Martin Brown and Brian Howe and argued there was no doubt these two deaths were connected and shared the same killer - or killers as he was suggesting in this case. The prosecution pointed out that after the death of Martin Brown, which was initially judged to be an accident by the police medical examiner, Mary Bell had made references to other children and families of Martin being strangled. Mr Lyons asked how it was that Mary Bell was able to anticipate the precise nature of Martin's death when that fact was still a long way from being established? Mr Lyons drew a distinction between Mary and Norma and made it clear that, in the view of the prosecution, Mary was the more dominant and cunning of the two girls.

Mary Bell sat blank faced as this was going on and she would maintain that blankness for much of the trial - or most of it anyway. This was largely taken as evidence that she was a black void with no emotions. Mary Bell later claimed the truth was less existential. She said she decided not to smile or show emotion out of respect for the gravity of the case. That would have been a nice gesture were it not for the fact she was one who had murdered the two boys. During his opening speech, Mr Lyons also told the court about how Mary and Norma had broken into the Woodlands Crescent nursery twice, the first time leaving notes confessing to the murder of Martin Brown. Hand-writing experts, said M r Lyons, had established that both Mary and Norma were involved in writing the notes. Mr Lyons also told the court how Mary and Norma had pestered the grieving family of Martin Brown and asked them 'morbid' questions about Martin purely for their own amusement. During the trial the prosecution also let the court know that a boy named David McCready had testified that he witnessed Mary Bell declare herself to be a murderer and then point to the row of houses near where Brian Howe was found.

Ron Wright, a detective for Northumbria Police at the time, described Norma as looking 'nonplussed' in court as if she had no idea what was going on. Wright described Mary Bell as looking 'alert' during the trial and giving the impression of having a much better grasp of the situation than Norma. The perception of Mary Bell as highly intelligent gained a lot of its traction from her performance in court. While her police statements and lack of criminal nous had often been, well, childish, in court she displayed an ability to think on her feet and was confident and brisk with her answers. At one point, Mary even pointed out to a QC and the judge that they had muddled up Martin Brown and Brian Howe on a specific point. They all had to stop and then realised Mary Bell was right. Mr

Wright said his main memory of the trial was the histrionic performance of Betty Bell in the public gallery. She sobbed, sighed, gasped, made audible comments, and at one point performed a dramatic and theatrical exit only to return (in equally theatrical style) back to her seat just a few minutes later.

Most of the court was fascinated by the off stage drama supplied by Betty Bell and often turned to look at her. The exception to this was Mary Bell. Mary displayed no interest whatsoever in her mother's antics. Mary Bell later said she couldn't face looking at her mother because she was the reason why her family were in court having to go through this horrible ordeal. Mary felt ashamed and knew her mother was angry at her. Whether or not Mary Bell really felt ashamed is hard to answer. The eleven year-old girl in court didn't look or act very ashamed. Mary listened very carefully to the long opening statement by Rudolph Lyons QC. Mr Lyons told the court about the nursery sandpit incident where Mary had tried to strangle two girls - stuffing sand in the mouth of one of them. Even more damaging than that was Mr Lyons telling the court that fibres from Mary's cotton skirt had been found on both Martin Brown and Brian Howe. Mary had told the police that she didn't play with Martin Brown the day of his death. If that was the case how could fibres from her clothes have ended up on him?

The court heard (from Norman Lee, who was the chief scientific officer at the forensics lab) that fibres from Norma's clothes were found on Brian Howe but not Martin Brown. The upshot of this was that, though both girls were still a long way from the shore, Mary Bell was in significantly deeper water than Norma. Norma was the first of the two girls to go into bat in court. She had to swear on the Bible that she would tell the truth. Norma had to give evidence for five hours and it soon became apparent this was not a task she was equipped to do. Norma was almost unrecognisable from the girl who usually milled around the ruined streets of Scotswood's slum clearances and the Tin Lizzie. Her hair had been freshly washed for court and her mother made sure she scrubbed her face clean. Her shoes sparkled with polish and she had a neat and clean cotton dress on. Norma did not look like a killer or a criminal street urchin. The best way to describe Norma in court would be terrified. She looked like she didn't belong there - which was a huge advantage to her as far as impressions go.

Norma was asked by her QC about the time when two girls were attacked in the nursery sandpit. Norma's responses to questions in court were hesitant and timid. It was hard work to get anything out of her because she was so nervous and shy. Although court two was supposed to be the smaller court it wasn't that much smaller than the main court and the judge still sat high above looming down over everyone. Prompted by her patient QC Mr Smith, Norma said she had been very scared when Mary attacked Pauline Watson in the sandpit. Norma told the court, in not much more than a whisper, that Mary had used both hands when she squeezed Pauline Watson's neck. Mary Bell always denied the sandpit incident. She insisted in court that she was behind a toy hut and had nothing to do with the attack. Without explicitly saying as much, Mary seemed to imply that Norma was more to blame than her for the sandpit trouble. The trial also heard evidence from Norma's parents that they had banned Mary Bell from playing with their daughter Susan after they caught Mary attempting to throttle Susan after a disagreement between the two children.

Norma seemed innocent and frightened in court and this transmitted to the jury. The evidence was also far less damning for Norma than it was for Mary. This is not to say though that everyone was happy at the way Norma walked free after this case and was never convicted for anything. There were a few police officers (though the minority) and also a few 'experts' who felt Norma should have got some sort of conviction. Norma was present at the second murder and went back to visit the body twice. She took part in the nursery vandalism and notes and may have taken part in the mutilation of Brian's body. Was she quite as innocent as she made out? The jury, the only people who mattered at this specific time, clearly DID think Norma was as innocent in real life as she appeared in court. Norma was asked by Mr Lyons if Mary Bell had ever demonstrated to her how little children could be killed. The timid and confused Norma had to be prompted into answering the question by the judge. It wouldn't be the last time this happened during her questioning. Norma eventually said she had seen Mary Bell demonstrate how to kill children. Mr Lyons suggested this a 'naughty' thing for Mary Bell to have done. Norma, after more prompting, was guided into agreeing with Mr Lyons.

R. P. Smith QC now asked Norma some questions about Martin Brown. There was a distressed and pained look on Norma's face when Martin Brown was mentioned. It suddenly became even more difficult to prompt her into responding to the questions. Mr Smith, after some effort, got Norma to state that she had seen Martin Brown on the day he died both before and after she had dinner at home. Norma said she had seen Martin Brown with some workmen in St Margaret's Road. One of the workmen, a Mr Hall, actually gave evidence at the trial. When some boys out getting firewood found Martin in the house the first thing they had done was run to tell these workmen because they were the nearest adults. The workmen had tried to revive Martin Brown. Earlier in the day Martin Brown had passed by the workmen and they had given him some of their packed lunch. What happened later was very upsetting to the workmen because the tragedy involved this friendly little boy who they'd been kind to earlier. Norma told the court that the last time she saw Martin was when he was being taken away in the ambulance.

Norma was asked a lot of questions about sightings and times in relation to the two victims and this got somewhat confusing - not least for Norma. Norma also kept referring to Mary Bell as 'May' in court - which initially confused the judge and the QC's (though not Mary's of course) because they had no idea that Mary Bell was always called 'May' by everyone she knew. In the end, the kind and clever judge picked up on this and called Mary Bell by the name May when he wanted to prompt her on something. The questions moved to the incident where Mary and Norma attempted to get inside the derelict house where Martin had been found to take a look. Norma told the court that they didn't manage to get very far inside before a workman told them off and ordered them to go back outside. Norma told her QC that by this stage a small crowd of children had started to gather. It seems that news travelled fast when it came to kids in Scotswood in 1968.

Norma told the court that the adults were trying to identify the boy who had been found and it was actually Mary Bell who volunteered and therefore probably identified Martin Brown for them. Norma couldn't say this for sure because she didn't go into the house herself. She merely saw Mary Bell go in. Norma got tearful a few times talking about Martin Brown. She certainly wasn't faking this. Norma was genuinely upset. Mary Bell gave her evidence in court in a more matter of fact way than Norma and did not seem visibly distressed having to talk about this stuff. One can see why the jury's instincts were considerably more sympathetic when it came to Norma. Mr Smith asked Norma about Mary Bell then seeking out Rita Finlay to tell her that Martin had had an accident. Norma confirmed that this had happened and Mr Smith left it at that. At the trial, Norma was also asked about the nursery vandalism and confession notes which had been left there. Norma said it was all Mary Bell's idea and they had written the notes together in Mary's house.

Norma said each of them would contribute part of a word

or alternate writing letters - which explained why the notes were such an eccentric scrawl. As she gave her evidence, Norma would often turn back and look towards her mother (Catherine) like a sort of silent plea for her mother to rescue her from this nightmare and take her home. Norma's mother, who was close enough to talk to Norma, would gently tell Norma to face the judge. Norma's mother was confident that her daughter was innocent of the charges and needed only to tell the truth. If she did that this ordeal would be over very soon and they could take Norma home and leave Mary Bell to her own fate. Norma would also glance at Mary Bell when she gave her evidence. It was as if she wanted to keep track of Mary's reactions.

Norma got upset again when she was forced to talk about Brian Howe. Sometimes her answers were little more than whispers and everyone would find themselves almost leaning in to try and pick up what she had said. The judge would often have to repeat what Norma had said out loud just to make sure the jury knew what her answer had been. Norma said that Mary Bell 'pinched' Brian Howe's nose and asked her to take 'over' (in effect finish him off) when she had been 'hurting' him for a time. Norma told the court that she had fled in horror at this point. Her only real defence why she didn't report this or stop Mary Bell was to say that Brian was still alive when she left. Norma said she had no idea that Mary was going to kill Brian Howe. She thought Mary was just being rough and a bully. Norma said that Mary had stopped hurting Brian Howe 'for a bit' when she left so she didn't think Brian was in danger. Norma told the court that never once did she touch Brian Howe during this incident.

The trial was a big contributing factor to the perception of Norma Joyce Bell as someone who wasn't very bright. Her confusion and inability to provide quick answers was plain to see. In hindsight though we understand that Norma was on trial for murders she did not commit so her confusion was genuine. She had no idea what happened to Martin Brown but she was being charged with his murder and being asked questions about his death. As a result of this, Norma in court was like watching someone stumble around in the dark. She had no idea what was happening. Mary Bell on the other hand was guilty. She was being charged with two murders that she knew more about than anyone. Her only option was to go on the front foot.

Norma was reluctant to talk and didn't really need to anyway (her confusion and tears, though unwitting and genuine, proved to be a winning combination because it made the jury feel sorry for her) but Mary Bell had no choice. Mary had to talk if she was to have any chance of digging herself out of this hole. She had to provide convincing answers and do some dodging and deflecting. Mary Bell, for the most part, managed to do this. In the end it was to no avail and tripped herself up by trying to be too clever. Mary Bell was also unaware that her lack of emotion was not playing well in court. It was though a confident performance and a sharp contrast to Norma. Mary Bell didn't realise though that this was merely another nail in her own legal coffin. When the jury had heard from both of the defendants it was pretty clear to them that Mary Bell was the brains of the organisation. They saw Mary Bell as the dominant personality and Norma as the clueless sidekick.

FANNY AND FAGGOT

Dr Robert Orton, a psychiatrist who interviewed Mary in custody, testified at the trial for the defence (of Mary Bell). He said Mary Bell was suffering from a psychopathic personality. As we discussed in a previous chapter, when boiled right down, this basically means a person who has no feelings or regard for fellow human beings. This would explain why Mary

Bell, after killing the boys, was able to happily resume her normal life without an ounce of remorse or guilt. Dr Ian Frazer of Prudhoe Monkton Mental Hospital also testified at the trial for Norma's defence. Dr Frazer's role was basically to say that Norma wasn't very intelligent. He said Norma had never shown any signs of aggression in custody and though her understanding of right and wrong was limited she was well aware that it was wrong to kill.

Though we have no way of knowing for sure it seems likely that Mary Bell probably would have killed another child in the end if she hadn't been arrested. This would have tipped her over into full blown serial killer status. The expert view that Mary was 'subnormal' meant that if she was found guilty it would be manslaughter as a result of diminished responsibility. The court was fuller than normal when Mary Bell was called to give evidence. Mary was the person who the press corps turned up to see. Mary Bell was aware of this increased 'buzz' and attendance when her turn to speak came. She knew by now she was the main focus of this trial and that Norma had been relegated to the part of supporting actor. Norma was half-way home but Mary hadn't even got on the bus yet and probably never would.

The night before she gave evidence, Mary Bell confided to a police officer (female police officers were assigned to watch over Mary Bell in custody) that she was gloomy about the outcome of the trial. Mary said Norma was seen as 'daft' (stupid) and so wouldn't get blamed for anything. Mary Bell, as with Norma, had to swear on the Bible that she would tell the truth in court. Asked if she knew about God and religion by the judge, Mary said she sometimes went to the 'mission'. There was a mission church in Benwell very close to Mary Bell. A mission church is one that does not have full status but is supported by the community and wider groups and seeks to spread the Christian faith. Mary Bell often carried a Bible around with her and according to her family spent a lot of time reading it. It turned out though that she used the Bible as a sort of scrapbook to keep a record of which of her relatives had died. That was a perfect illustration of young Mary Bell's strange character. Even when she was assumed to be doing something normal or nice there was usually some morbid or sinister undertone.

Harvey Robson QC asked Mary Bell about fibres from her clothes being found on Martin Brown despite the fact that she told the police she didn't play with him the day he died.

Mary Bell answered this by saying she didn't play with Martin Brown that day but she did give him a few pushes on a swing. This was a very sharp answer but maybe too sharp for its own good. Mary Bell was suggesting that giving someone a push on a swing and playing are two different things. She did not regard giving Martin Brown a 'swing' to be playing. With this answer Mary Bell had provided an explanation for the fibres and a counter to the assumption that she had lied to the police about not playing with Martin Brown. The only problem was that Mary Bell now appeared to 'winging it' and adjusting her evidence on the fly.

Mary Bell, in relation to her trip to the derelict house at 85 St Margaret's Road where Martin Brown was found, gave evidence which was at odds with the timeline established by Norma. This was not only confusing but added to the perception that Mary Bell was making a lot of this up. Her answers were snappy and quick and if she didn't understand a question she say would so and have the question put to her a different way. Mary Bell also had a habit, a tactic if you were being cynical, of straying off the subject and rambling on about things like her cat or playing the recorder - details which were irrelevant to the question she had been asked. The theory is that Mary Bell did this to calm her nerves, give herself time to think, and to avoid giving a straight answer to tricky questions. Whenever she wandered off on one of these verbal rambles she was steered back to the topic at hand by whichever QC was asking her questions.

It was Mary's confidence and quick answers which made her seem way more intelligent than Norma. Though she is sometimes depicted as being sullen and truculent all through the trial this wasn't the case at all. Mary was polite (framing her responses with 'sir' at all times) and even genial at times in her interactions with the judge and QC. The problem with this is that there was, or is, an expectation for a child in this situation to show more emotion. Norma had cried and got upset when she had to talk about Martin Brown and Brian Howe. Mary Bell did not show any sadness when she had to do the same. Mary's account of the day Martin Brown died soon began to diverge from what Norma had told the court. Mary Bell said she and Norma had gone to the shop at the top of their street to buy some dog food and then Norma had gone off with the dog food while Mary went up to the house where Martin Brown was found. Mary said she had heard from other people in the street that there had been an accident so she decided to walk up to have a look.

Mary said she went in the house and saw Martin Brown in the arms of a workman. She then decided to go back and fetch Norma. Mary Bell's evidence contradicted the evidence given by two of the workmen during the trial. Mary Bell was confident and articulate in court but her intelligence was superficial. Her actual words often had the opposite effect to what she had intended and Mary Bell never quite seemed to grasp this fact. Mary Bell's details continued to be quite different from what Norma had told the court. Mary said that she and Norma tried to get the derelict house to see what was going on but a boy told them to get out when they were on the stairs so they had to leave. Mary said this was when they went to find Rita Finlay to tell her about the accident. Rita, according to Mary Bell, didn't believe her but a local woman named Mrs Carver then confirmed this so Rita ran to the house where Martin was. Mary Bell said she ran after Rita.

Harvey Robson QC asked Mary Bell if she had done anything to harm Martin Brown when he was alive that day. Mary Bell shook her head and said she hadn't. Mr Robson then asked Mary Bell if at any point she had been inside 85 St Margaret's Road with Martin Brown when he was alive. Once again Mary Bell replied by saying that she hadn't. Mary Bell was asked why she drawn a bottle of tablets next to Martin Brown lying down in her school notebook. At the time of her illustration the empty tablet bottles in the house had not been disclosed in public. Mary said she heard rumours about a tablet bottle being in the room where Martin died. Asked how she thought Martin had died, Mary Bell replied by saying that she thought he had perhaps fallen through the roof after climbing up there.

Things got tougher for Mary Bell when she was questioned by Mr Lyons for the prosecution. Mr Lyons wanted to know why Mary had told members of the Howe family that Norma had strangled Martin Brown. This was how Martin Brown had died but that information was not known to anyone at the time - not even the police. Mary Bell replied by saying she had fallen out with Norma that day and simply said something mean about her. Mary said that she couldn't think of anything else to say at the time. Mary Bell was asked if she knew that Martin Brown really had been strangled at the time she made that comment. Mary replied by saying no. She had no idea Martin Brown had died or how he had died when she made that comment. Mr Lyons asked Mary Bell why she had told the Howe family that Norma grabbed Martin Brown by the throat. He wanted to know why Mary had mentioned the throat. Was there any specific reason why this came into her head?

As a prelude to this question Mr Lyons had got Mary Bell to agree with him that there were many different ways one might harm a little boy. So why did she mention the throat? Mary Bell said it was inspired by something she saw in Apache on television. Apache is a 1954 Western film starring Burt

Lancaster but it could be the case that Mary was talking about a Western television show (of which there were many in the 1950s and 1960s) and 'Apache' was her catch-all term. Mr Lyons pointed out that there must have been many other incidents of violence in things Mary had watched on television so why not pick one of those - like someone being hit on the head? Mary replied by saying that being hit on the head just knocks people down and doesn't kill them. Though she managed to come up with quick responses, Mr Lyons had Mary Bell on the ropes with this line of questioning. She did not provide a satisfactory explanation for why she had seemed to anticipate or know the manner of Martin Brown's death. The best Mary Bell could do was to imply it was merely a strange coincidence.

Mary Bell had a solicitor named David Bryson who sat next to her during the trial. Bryson was appointed as her solicitor around the time she had to do a number of police interviews in relation to Brian Howe's death. Bryson's main job in court was to explain to Mary Bell what was happening. Mary Bell would later say that she didn't think her legal team in court did a very good job. It is doubtful though that anyone could have saved Mary Bell in that courtroom. The best they might have done is got a different sort of sentence. After the trial, Mary Bell's solicitors, Septimus Ward and Rose Ltd, appealed against her sentence. They wanted it changed to a hospital treatment order. A hospital order can be given by the criminal courts instead of a custodial sentence if the defendant has a mental disorder and requires treatment in hospital. Perhaps this is what disappointed Mary Bell. The fact that she got sent to juvenile detention institutions and then prison. Mary Bell was not actually eligible for a hospital order at her her trial because she was too young.

Mr Lyons asked Mary Bell about telling Mr Dobson at the police station that she had never played with Martin Brown. Mary Bell was a little foggy on this all of a sudden but in the end agreed with Mr Lyons that she had said that. When pressed on this point Mary Bell said she had not played with Martin Brown but had given him a quick swing. Mr Lyons asked if she told Mr Dobson about the swing. Mary Bell said she hadn't. She was back to her sly gambit that giving someone a quick swing is not the same thing as playing with them. Mr Lyons asked Mary Bell if she had changed her evidence and invented the swing because the trial evidence mentioned that fibres from her clothes were found on Martin Brown? Mary Bell denied this and simply said no. The court heard from handwriting expert Roland Page about the confession notes left in the Woodlands Crescent nursery. Mr Page said it was almost impossible to say which girl was responsible for specific words or letters except to say that they probably both had a hand in them.

The prosecution argued that the confession notes were an admission of guilt and should be taken as such. The two defence QC's argued that the notes were a silly and immature - if bad taste - prank by the girls and should not be treated as evidence of guilt. Harvey Robson QC asked Mary Bell about the confession notes left in the nursery. Mary Bell said the notes were a 'joint idea' that she and Norma came up with. Norma had found a red biro and they were doing some drawing so they they came up with the idea of doing the notes. Mary said it was Norma's idea to break into the nursery again. Mary Bell then gave a long account of how they had climbed over a barbed wire fence and then got into the nursery through a trap door on the roof. Mary said they found keys in the nursery which they used to open all the locked doors. They, according to Mary, came up with new notes while in the nursery.

Mary Bell seemed to indicate that they had composed two notes in her house. Four were left in the nursery in the end. Mary Bell said they broke into the nursery because they thought it would be a great 'joke' to play. Norma's barrister R.

P. Smith QC asked Mary Bell why exactly Norma thought it would be a great 'joke' to break into the nursery.

It was at this point that Mary Bell upped the stakes. She said Norma wanted to get 'put away'. Mary said that Norma wanted to run away and get put in a home so that she could avoid the police and kill the 'little ones'. Mr Justice Cusack peered down at Mary Bell with a confused look on his face. He asked Mr Smith what Mary Bell had just said. Mr Smith repeated Mary Bell's comments that Norma wanted to run away so she could murder the 'little ones'. Mr Justice Cusack seemed to sigh wearily and then suggested it was time to adjourn for a while.

Mary Bell, so far largely unflappable, finally and for some unknown reason lost her cool at this moment in the trial. She began shouting threats at Norma and had to be restrained by a female police officer. Norma's family, though shocked initially, must have been delighted by this sudden display of anger. The jury had just seen evidence of Mary Bell's temper and unpredictability for themselves. The pressure of the trial finally got to Mary Bell in that moment. All of her composure suddenly went in an instant.

Norma was called to give evidence again in relation to the nursery notes and questioned by Mr Lyons. Of particular interest was the line 'I murder so THAT I may come back'. Norma was asked what this meant and if she wrote that line. It certainly would have been interesting to hear an explanation or analysis from Norma on this curious line but sadly none was forthcoming. Norma soon started sobbing again. She couldn't answer any questions - except to deny that she thought Martin Brown's death was an amusing joke.

Mr Justice Cusack asked Mr Lyons if there was some other way to approach this line of questioning. The judge could see the distress of Norma and he had a duty to protect the child. He also though had a duty to allow Mr Lyons to ask questions in court. You can see then how this trial had become a tricky and wearing task for Mr Justice Cusack. He must have been glad when it was all over. The judge, in apologetic fashion, told Mr Lyons that it wouldn't do to have a weeping child being badgered with cross-examination questions. Mr Justice Cusack said the jury would have to decide if Norma's weeping and distress was genuine or simply because she wanted to avoid difficult questions which harmed her defence. One of the newspaper reports of the case at this time described Norma as a 'pathetic child' completely 'overwhelmed' by the trial.

Mary Bell was also questioned on the nursery notes again by Mr Lyons. Asked who was responsible for each specific note or line, Mary said she had no idea. She had calmed down by now and regained her composure. Mary Bell was asked what 'Fanny and Faggot' was a reference to in the nursery notes they had written. Mary said these were just fictional nicknames she and Norma had given themselves. During the trial Mary Bell was also questioned on why she had asked Martin Brown's mother if she could look in his coffin. Mary said she was engaged in a game of 'chicken' with Norma over who could say the most daring thing. Mary Bell conceded that this was childish and in poor taste.

The jury was made up of five women and seven men. This was a horrible trial for which to be called up for jury duty. The members of the jury had to look at post mortem photographs of the two dead victims and listen to some highly distressing evidence. Home Office pathologist Bernard Knight was among those called to testify and his evidence was unbearably sad. After her sudden outburst, Mary Bell managed to complete her duties at the trial in the calm and polite fashion she had managed for most of it. While she had impressed everyone with her verbal fluency and concentration levels the trial as a whole had not gone that well for her. Norma had come across in court as much more sympathetic and way less intelligent than Mary Bell. Mary Bell's private prediction that 'daft'

Norma would get off the hook turned out to be completely on the mark.

Doli incapax was a factor in this trial. Doli incapax is a legal doctrine that refers to the presumption that a child is incapable of committing a crime due to a lack of understanding of the consequences of their actions. This concept is often applied in criminal law, particularly in cases involving minors. The principle holds that very young children, typically those under a certain age (often around ten), are presumed to be incapable of forming the intent necessary to commit an offense, and thus cannot be held criminally liable for their actions. The prosecution therefore were supposed to prove that Mary Bell and Norma had intent and (crucially) knew what they were doing when they (allegedly) committed these crimes.

THE DEMON CHILD

By far the most dramatic part of Mary Bell's evidence came when she alleged that Norma killed Brian Howe. Mary said she was unable to move when this happened and when Norma attacked Brian it felt like there was 'glue' trapping her on the spot. Mary Bell said that Norma told Brian to lie down and wait for the woman to come along with the sweets. This part of Mary Bell's evidence was more or less the same as what she had said in her police statement. Mary Bell was asked in court if Norma had used one or two hands in the attack but said she couldn't remember. Mary Bell told the court that she tried to pull Norma from Brian Howe but Norma screamed at her loudly and refused to stop.

This evidence was not very convincing on a number of levels. An obvious weakness is that there was a row of houses quite close to the Tin Lizzie and also a group of boys playing in the vicinity that afternoon and yet the police did not encounter a single witness who reported hearing a child's scream that day. Mary used the witness bench to demonstrate how Norma had strangled Brian Howe. Mary said that Norma was also banging Brian's head on a piece of wood as she did this and her fingertips had turned white from the force and pressure. Mary Bell said she did not report Brian Howe's murder out of misplaced loyalty to Norma. Norma started crying during Mary Bell's evidence on Brian Howe and could be heard saying "I never!" over and over. In his closing speech for the prosecution, Rudolph Lyons QC said Norma was a 'simple backward girl' of feeble intelligence. He described Mary Bell as vicious, cruel, cunning and abnormal. Mr Lyons said that the cunning of Mary Bell was terrifying. She was, in the words of Mr Lyons, an 'evil and compelling influence' on a par with the fictional Svengali.

In his own closing remarks, Norma's barrister R. P. Smith QC told the jury that there was no evidence to link Norma to these murders. The only evidence against Norma was the words of Mary Bell and Mary Bell, Mr Smith told the jury, was an unreliable witness whose only concern was to save her own skin by pretending Norma had done these crimes. Mr Smith told the jury that they must separate these two girls and remove the anger and annoyance they must have fostered hearing about these murders. Mr Smith said the jury must banish the instinct to punish both of these girls. They must only punish the guilty party - Mary Bell. Harvey Robson QC, who was defending Mary Bell, had the hardest task in his closing statement. Mr Robson said that in Mary's mind there was a 'no man's land' between 'reality and fancy'. Just because Mary Bell pretended to be a murderer to other kids or left childish confession notes in a nursery it didn't mean that she had really done these terrible things in reality.

In his closing remarks to the jury, Mr Justice Cusack said to them - "And you above all, in reaching your decisions, must be governed, not by hearts but by your heads, and that is an important thing to have in mind. There has been, of course, every kind of emotion in this case, and everybody who has listened to it, must have been subject to astonishment, dismay, horror, pity. Put all that aside. Judge the case only on the facts as you find them to be, having listened to the evidence. Don't be swayed either by sympathy for the two girls who are so young and find themselves on so serious a charge, or by sympathy for the parents and relations of those two little boys who lost their lives tragically, whoever or whatever may have been the cause of their deaths." The fate of Mary and Norma was now in the hands of the jury. It was just a week away from Christmas 1968. Although the trial only lasted nine days everyone involved was mightily relieved when it was over. It must have felt a lot longer than nine days to Mary and Norma. All that remained now was for everyone to return for the verdict.

The jury retired on the 17th of December and took four hours to reach their decision. Mary Bell was cleared of murder but found guilty of manslaughter on diminished grounds. Norma was acquitted of all charges. Mary Bell's family were distraught. Her grandmother started crying and Billy Bell put his head in his hands. Mary became tearful and had to be comforted by her solicitor. The reaction of Norma and her family to the verdict was the polar opposite. When she was found not guilty, Norma was so delighted she started clapping. Mary Bell was given an indefinite sentence of imprisonment. This meant she was going to be locked up for quite a while. How long that would be was unknown. Norma could look forward to Christmas with her family while Mary could look forward only to custody and uncertainty. Once her tears subsided, Mary Bell looked rather confused. She didn't know what this all meant and what was going to happen to her. Dr David Westbury, a Home Office psychiatrist, informed the jury that Mary had a psychopathic disorder within the meaning of the Mental Health Act. Asked by the judge if he knew of a place where she could go, he said, "No". Questioned by Mr Harvey Robson for Mary, Dr Westbury said he thought her period of treatment should last "some years".

In his sentencing remarks, Mr Justice Cusack said - "The child need not stand and I shall address myself to the matters without specifically addressing myself to her. On the verdict of the Jury in this case, Mary Bell has been found guilty on two counts of manslaughter. The verdict is one of manslaughter because the jury found that at the material time she had diminished responsibility. Otherwise their verdict would have been one of murder. In the result it means that this child, now aged only eleven, has in fact been found to have killed two other children. My difficulty is to know what order should now be made by the court. Having regard to the medical evidence put before me, I should have been willing to make . a hospital order, so that she could have been taken to a mental institution to receive the appropriate treatment . accompanied . by a restriction order . which would have meant that she could not have been released from a hospital without. special. authority.

"Unhappily, I am not able to make such an order because one of the requirements of the Mental Health Act is that I must be satisfied, firstly, that there is a hospital to which she could go; secondly, that she could be admitted to that institution within twenty-eight days. Evidence has been given to me by Dr. Westbury . that it has been impossible to find any institution to which she can be admitted for treatment under the Mental Health Act . The responsible Government Department requires time to consider what they wish to do . I make no criticism of that Department. But it is a most unhappy thing that, with all the resources of this country, whether it be the Ministry of Social Security, or the Home Office, it appears that no hospital is available which is suitable for the accommodation of this girl and to which she could be admitted.

"All the requirements, apart from the one I have mentioned, of the Mental Health Act have been satisfied, and I am merely precluded from doing what I would otherwise do by the fact that no such hospital is available. No evidence has been put before me which would enable me, therefore, to make an order of the kind I would wish to make. I must, therefore, turn to other matters. If this had been the case of an adult, having regard to the evidence put before me, which I fully accept, that this is a child who is dangerous, I should have felt obliged to impose a life sentence for the reason that, not only did the gravity of the of fences warrant it, but that there was evidence of mental disease or abnormality which made it impossible to determine the date when the person concerned could be safely released.

"It is an appalling thing that, in a child as young as this, one has to determine such matters, but I am entirely satisfied that, anxious as I am to do everything for her benefit, my primary duty is to protect other people for the reasons that I have indicated. I take the view that there is a very grave risk to other children if. she is not closely watched and every conceivable step taken to see that she does not do again what it has been found that she did do. In the case of a child of this age no question of imprisonment arises, but I have the power to order a sentence of detention, and it seems to me that no other method of dealing with her, in the circumstances, is suitable.

"I therefore have to turn to what length of detention should be imposed. I say at once that, if an un determinate period is imposed, as in the case of a life sentence of imprisonment, that does not mean that the person concerned is kept in custody indefinitely, or for the rest of their natural lives. It means that the position can be considered from time to time and, if it becomes safe to release that person, that person can be released. For that reason the sentence of the court concurrently in respect of these two matters upon Mary

Bell is a sentence of detention and the detention will be for life. The child Mary Bell may be taken out of court." As for Norma, the judge said he hoped that no one ever attempted to discuss these matters with her again and it was in her best interests to put this affair behind her. The judge said he was 'anxious' about Norma's future and hoped she would now be left in peace to get on with her life.

The court had been fuller than usual for the verdict and sentencing. There were even some foreign press who had come to file reports on this strange and horrible case where two young girls were on trial for killing children. When the trial wound to a close the court slowly emptied. That final day was the last time Mary Bell and Norma ever saw each other. Fanny & Faggot were no more. Although it was a painful and terrifying ordeal for her, the trial could not have gone much better for Norma. The people in court felt protective of Norma when she kept crying and they saw no evidence that this child was a liar and killer - as Mary Bell portrayed her to be.

Mary Bell on the other hand, due in large part to the perspicacity of her remarks in court, was seen as the cunning manipulator and the colder personality of the two girls. And it wasn't just a case of the jury not liking the look of Mary Bell and distrusting her more than Norma. The evidence heard during the case pointed directly towards Mary Bell. She was the only defendant with forensic links to both victims. She was the defendant with a history of grabbing kids by the neck. Martin Brown's mother June, when she heard about the verdict, considered the sentence to be fair. It sounded about right to her. June said she loathed Mary Bell with every fibre of her being and would have happily killed Mary Bell at the time if left alone with her. June also despised Norma. Even though Norma was found innocent, June could never forgive Norma for her part in the tasteless nursery notes about Martin.

Mary Bell's cluelessness on what would happen to her now

was shared by the authorities. They didn't even know where they were supposed to take her. After she left the courtroom she was allowed to say a temporary goodbye to her family. Betty kissed Mary Bell - something she rarely did. Billy Bell gave Mary a hug. It hadn't yet dawned on Mary Bell that her life had now undergone a sliding doors moment. Instead of being little May Bell of 70 Whitehouse House, playing with her dog and going to school, she was now Mary Bell - notorious incarcerated child killer. Mary Bell was now the 'Demon Child' and 'Bad Seed' in the media. For a week at least until the news cycle moved onto other matters, she was one of the most famous people in the country. In the news in 1968, British Rail ran their last steam train service, the M1 motorway was completed, Enoch Powell made his controversial 'Rivers of Blood' speech, Mauritius became independent from Britain, Manchester United won the European Cup, the comedian Tony Hancock committed suicide, and the Olympics took place in Mexico City with Great Britain winning five gold medals. The case of Mary Bell earned as much ink as most of these stories.

As a very temporary measure, Mary Bell was taken to a remand home in Brasside, County Durham. This institution was built in 1965 and was later expanded to become Low Newton Prison. Among the famous figures who later spent time at Low Newton Prison are Rose West, Lucy Letby, Joanna Dennehy, and Sharon Carr (who, as we discussed in a previous chapter, would become Britain's youngest killer). Mary Bell's days at the remand home were a holding operation until it was worked out what to do with her. Mary's solicitors later complained that she was being pushed 'from pillar to post' because of the lack of facilities for her. They were also irritated when some press photographers took photos outside their building.

The lack of any obvious place to send Mary Bell exposed a weakness in the system but then you can't really blame the authorities in 1968 for not having a special system in place explicitly designed to process eleven year-old girls who murder younger children. Mary Bell was a ghastly anomaly suddenly thrown at them. An unexpected and unwelcome puzzle to solve. The only thing that everyone agreed on was that Mary Bell needed to go somewhere where she would get an education and supervision. If you convict a 35 year-old serial killer then that person is pretty much considered a lost cause who must be taken out of society - quite likely forever. An eleven year-old girl who has killed is an entirely different matter. A child has the real possibility of rehabilitation.

No one is the same person as an adult as they are at eleven. This doesn't always mean they become a much better person (look at Jon Venables, one of the killers of James Bulger, who is now back in prison for incessantly downloading indecent images of children) but you have to give them the chance. Mary Bell would be given that chance now. It was up to her to make the best of it and prove she was capable of changing. The most obvious immediate punishment Mary Bell suffered for her crimes was the loss of her teenage years. She never experienced what it was like to be an ordinary teenager. Her teens were spent in juvenile detention and prison. The frightening thing is though that if she hadn't killed Brian Howe she would have got away with Martin Brown's murder. If she hadn't killed Brian she wouldn't be in custody at all.

NORMA

Norma Joyce Bell went back to Whitehouse Road after the trial. The perception that Norma only got into trouble when she was with Mary Bell turned out to be true. Now released from her role as Mary Bell's sidekick, Norma never got into trouble again. She was suddenly a benign and unthreatening presence to other children and young teenagers. Norma was on probation and warned about her future conduct but she never gave the authorities any reason to regret releasing her. Norma was also subject to what was called 'psychiatric supervision' for quite a while. This was because she had witnessed the attack on Brian Howe but then, instead of telling anyone about it or helping Brian, had wandered off to have her tea and play with other kids. By any standards that was seriously odd behaviour.

Norma's participation in the nursery vandalism and confession notes was also a blot on her copybook. Once she went home after the trial, Norma tried to get back to some sort of normality but it was not easy. She had been in custody for months and then had to endure the emotional rollercoaster of the trial. Norma found it strange and difficult to suddenly be thrown back into the life which was interrupted by the tragedies in Scotswood. What must have been strangest of all for Norma was not having Mary Bell two doors down. Despite all the bad blood between them in the end, the betrayal, and the knowledge that life without Mary Bell was for her own good, Norma still must have felt some sort of loss. Mary Bell had been her best friend but now they would never see other again. Norma staying out of trouble after the trial did tend to support the common theory that she had been in thrall to Mary Bell to the extent where it affected her ability to make rational decisions which were for her own good.

It must have been very strange for Norma to be back at Whitehouse Road and on the streets of Scotswood and yet never see Mary Bell anymore. She must have sometimes wondered, in her private thoughts and moments, where Mary Bell was and what she was now doing in custody. Not that Norma's feelings towards Mary Bell were all rose tinted. Norma was furious when Mary tried to blame her for the murders. The disturbing thing about this is that if Mary Bell's ruse had worked and Norma had been wrongly convicted for the murders one can't imagine Mary would have lost much sleep. Mary Bell didn't have normal feelings like guilt or empathy. It was the lack of these basic safety break emotions which made her capable of murder and capable of the most outrageous lies.

Norma went back to school and tried, as the judge had suggested at the trial in his summing up, to put the past behind her. There was some gossip about Norma at school, how she was a killer, but it was nothing Norma couldn't cope with. Norma came across as a shy and gentle girl in court but she wasn't a soft touch in real life. She wasn't scared of other kids. Norma was on her best behaviour though and didn't respond or get into any fights. Although she was cleared in court of having any role in the two murders, Norma was tarnished in the community by her past connections to Mary Bell. Norma tried to approach Martin Brown's mother June at one point to say hello and offer to babysit but June didn't want to know and snubbed her. Norma must have understood why June felt this way towards her but it still hurt.

Norma's presence around Scotswood was less prominent after the trial. She no longer had Mary Bell to knock around with and she was also nearly fourteen and getting too old to be playing street games with little kids. Norma therefore spent more time with her siblings and didn't go outside as much as she used to when Mary Bell was around. The fate of Norma is certainly a puzzle in the Mary Bell story because these two leading characters now diverged. Mary Bell's story would go on to have many twists and turns and generate national headlines decades on from her crimes but Norma's story more or less ended here. The rest of Norma's life is vague and was lived out of the spotlight. Her family never spoke to the press and neither did she. There are no articles on the internet from anyone who knew her.

Norma was a lot like someone who went into witness protection or changed their identity. She seemed to vanish.

We know that Norma's family moved away from Whitehouse Road in the end. A big factor in this decision was clearly the welfare of Norma. They wanted to get her away from old haunts where she was a notorious figure sometimes looked at with suspicion. It is said that the German magazine Stern actually did a feature on Norma after the trial but this article is elusive on internet archives. Stern (German for "Star) is a left leaning weekly current affairs magazine published in Hamburg. The magazine was founded in 1948 and is probably best known today for paying a large sum of money in 1983 for Adolf Hitler's diaries - which then turned out to be forged and merely a hoax. Stern included some of Norma's poetry in their magazine and she got some fan letters from Germans after the issue was published.

Although she was cleared of all charges in court, Norma's true crime connections to Mary Bell inevitably made her attractive to the strange people who yearn to be pen pals with criminals. It must have been a strange experience for Norma to get fan letters from abroad. A lot of these letters were probably too weird to respond to or enjoy but they were still fan letters in a loose sense. From what little we know of Norma, she left school with few qualifications and worked as a waitress. She is also believed to have got married and had a family at some point. There are stories that Norma got into trouble a little bit with the authorities because she kept talking about the trial and the Mary Bell case to people she knew. One of the terms of her release was that she wasn't supposed to blab about this stuff. It wasn't serious trouble though and she kept her nose clean (as Mary Bell would say) after the events of 1968.

The fact that Norma seemed to like talking about the Mary Bell case indicated that she had a degree of nostalgia for that time. Not the court case, the tragedies, or the betrayal, but more the days of wandering around with Mary Bell, making one another laugh, and living in their own private world of

Fanny & Faggot. Life must have seemed much simpler to her back then until Mary Bell destroyed everything and almost dragged Norma down with her. It is difficult to say how differently Norma may or may not have fared in a similar case today. Many believe that in a parallel case today Norma would have got some sort of conviction for assisting an offender or even assisting in a murder (though Norma obviously denied she had any role in Brian Howe's death).

Norma was technically an accessory to murder because she witnessed Mary Bell attacking Brian Howe and then viewed the body a couple of times without telling anyone what had happened. An adult would not have got away with doing this. If you witnessed a killer attacking someone and then went back to look at the body a few times without telling the police there had been a murder then you'd be looking at some prison time. What saved Norma was her age and the fact she was deemed to be simple minded in court and at Monkton Prudhoe Mental hospital. She was judged to be a gullible follower of Mary Bell and not an accomplice to murder. Some police detectives were suspicious of Norma and think it is possible she might have been a participant in the attack on Brian Howe. They were though in the minority and there is no clear evidence for this theory.

The only evidence against Norma was the claim of Mary Bell. We can dismiss this claim for one very obvious reason. Norma was not present when Martin Brown was murdered. This means that Mary Bell was trying to throw Norma under a bus to save herself. There is a theory that Mary Bell was suffering from Delusional Disorder. Delusional Disorder is a serious mental health condition marked by the presence of one or more delusions that persist for at least one month. These delusions are strongly held false beliefs that differ from reality, such as believing one is being persecuted, is under constant surveillance, or possesses exceptional abilities. Unlike schizophrenia, people with delusional disorder do not exhibit significant impairments in overall functioning and may even lead relatively normal lives outside of their delusional beliefs.

Mary's story that Norma was a killer may have been a symptom of these delusions. When she was in custody Mary went through a period where she invented an imaginary twin sister who she blamed for murdering Martin Brown and Brian Howe. In court though in 1968 it seems that Mary pretended Norma was a killer simply because it was her only option. She saw no other way of evading a guilty verdict. Long into her life, when she gave interviews to Gitta Sereny a book about her, Mary Bell seemed to display a barely concealed bitterness that she had been punished while Norma walked free from court. "The weaker makes the other stronger by being weak," Mary Bell would say of Norma many years later. Mary Bell seemed to blaming Norma for not stopping her. This seems to be a strange view of events given that Norma wasn't even there when Mary Bell murdered Martin Brown. Norma was present when Brian Howe was attacked but Mary Bell was the one who did the attacking. Norma wasn't to know that Mary Bell was going to kill him.

There was no compelling evidence that Norma was involved in Brian Howe's death. As such she ended up in this strange situation where she was put up a little pedestal of shame and infamy with Mary Bell but then taken down from it, dusted off, and sent home to go back to her normal mundane life. There are certainly stories that Norma struggled at times and had some mental health issues which were related to what she had seen and gone through in 1968. The available evidence, which was clear as day in court, is that Norma had feelings and was more empathetic than Mary Bell. This is what makes it unlikely that she played a direct part in Brian Howe's death. The community in Newcastle never really seemed to have any lingering dislike of Norma. They never blamed her for what happened.

When the relatives of Martin Brown and Brian Howe spoke to the press in years to come their ire was firmly targeted on Mary Bell. Norma was largely forgotten. June Richardson was rightly angry at Norma for the bad taste notes in the nursery and wanted nothing to do with her but she didn't blame Norma for Martin's death just as Eileen Corrigan didn't blame Norma for her son Brian Howe's death. They knew that Mary Bell was the one to blame. Norma was therefore a major character in the first act of the Mary Bell story, a co-lead in fact, but then written out of the next chapters once the trial ended. There was no role for Norma in the story anymore. She played no further part in the tale of Mary Bell and lived a quiet and private life out of the spotlight.

Had this all happened today you could perhaps, at a push, imagine a scenario where Norma wrote a book about her experience or appeared on This Morning talking about Mary Bell. But nothing like this happened and Norma faded out of sight. Unlike the incarcerated Mary Bell, Norma was able to live her teenage years as a normal person. She was able to take for granted things which were now denied to Mary Bell. Norma Bell was defined by being Mary Bell's sidekick. When she left that role she struggled to forge her own identity. Peter Moore, the first police officer to arrest Mary Bell (for the gas meter theft), said that when he spoke to Mary Bell and Norma it was Mary who did all the talking. Norma never said a word. She didn't have the sharpness and gift of the gab of Mary Bell so she accepted her role as the junior partner.

Norma Bell was though, when free of the company of Mary Bell, good at making friends. As we mentioned in a previous chapter, Rita Finlay (the aunt of Martin Brown) said that Norma was a 'lovely' girl who was impossible to dislike. This was evident in court - the jury and public gallery taking a shine to Norma but left cold by Mary Bell. With the weight of evidence on Norma's side too, Mary Bell stood no chance in court pitted against her friend. Maybe this what irked Mary

Bell about Norma - even long after they parted and had no contact anymore. She hated the fact that Norma was more popular than her. It was fine when they were friends and Mary Bell had Norma all to herself but Mary must have hated the thought of Norma out there alone, free and cleared of all charges, having a normal teenage life, meeting new people and getting on just fine without her.

We can only speculate on what might have happened if Mary Bell had not killed again after Martin Brown and so had never been arrested and convicted. Norma and Mary would likely have remained friends for at least a few more years but would this friendship have lasted into adulthood and beyond? Childhood friends, for a variety of reasons, often drift apart in teenage years or their early twenties. It seems logical to presume this would have happened to Norma and Mary in the end. We don't really know for sure though. It could be the case that their bond would have lasted a lot longer. The friendship of Norma and Mary brings to mind the words of the narrator in the film Stand By Me (which was based on Stephen King's novella The Body). "I never had any friends later on like the ones I had when I was twelve. Jesus, does anyone?"

The character that Norma unwittingly played when she was friends with Mary Bell vanished after the trial ended in December 1968. Norma now had to learn to be herself. The real Norma Joyce Bell was unassuming, quite shy, fond of writing poetry, and decent at heart. Norma had vindicated the jury who set her free. While she was not perfect and had done some horrible things in her time with Mary Bell the uneventful life of Norma after the trial seemed to confirm that Mary Bell had been a terrible influence. Left to her own devices Norma wasn't a bad person. When the trial ended Norma spent Christmas with her family and then began the adjustment to freedom as her teenage years stretched out before her. Mary Bell on the other hand faced a very different sort of challenge. Mary had to adjust to a new life in custody away from her family and Norma. Not only was she just eleven years-old, she was also one of the most notorious criminals in the country.

RED BANK

Just before Christmas 1968, Mary Bell was moved to Cumberlow Lodge in South Norwood, London. Cumberlow Lodge was a remand home for teenage girls. London must have felt like a million miles away to a staunch Geordie like Mary Bell. A statement released by the Home Office said that Mary Bell would stay at Cumberlow Lodge while the Home Secretary worked out what the best 'treatment' and 'care' for her would be. This is what prompted Mary's solicitors to complain that she was being pushed from pillar to post. As of yet there didn't seem to be much of a plan for what to do with Mary Bell. Cumberlow Lodge was a detention centre. It became a remand home in 1950 and was previously Lewisham Children's Home and Cumberlow Lodge Residential School. When it became public news that Mary Bell was at Cumberlow Lodge there were some complaints by the local community. The notion that Mary Bell was going to escape and start murdering local London children was silly but this was the sort of reaction she provoked.

Cumberlow Lodge was a huge place but there were less than a hundred girls there. Mary was in a unit with four other girls and shielded from the violence of the place (fights were common). Her solicitor David Bryson told the media that Mary was doing well and the Home Office said that visits by Mary Bell's parents were encouraged. Mary Bell had to attend school classes with a tutor while at Cumberlow Lodge but she wasn't there for long. A few months later Mary Bell was sent to Red Bank Secure Unit, a young offenders institution in

Newton-le-Willows, Merseyside. Red Bank later housed Jon Venables, one of the killers of James Bulger. Although her crimes were the worst thing you could imagine there was a sense of social responsibility to Mary Bell. Mary Bell became an interesting experiment for the authorities. She was the 'Bad Seed'. A demonic double killer. The people treating Mary Bell were fascinated to see if this notorious child could be rehabilitated and shaped into something more normal and human.

Red Bank was one of several English Local Authority Secure Children's Homes and opened in 1965. The young people there were detained under section 53 of the Children and Young Persons Act 1933. Mary Bell was still far too young to be sent to a prison. Mary was the only girl at Red Bank for most of the time. When they set up these Secure Children's Homes for serious young offenders it obviously never occurred to them they might have a killer girl on their hands one day. These sorts of places were founded with young boys in mind. The average person there was a teenage male who had been convicted for rape or arson or drugs offences. In later decades Red Bank became more of a specialist institution dealing with sex offenders but when Mary Bell was there it was more of a general place for all types of young offenders. Red Bank could be quite a rough place but Mary Bell was never someone to suffer from bullying. She was the type of girl who got the first punch in. Fairly soon she had a reputation at Red Bank for being quite volatile and so this made the other offenders think twice about annoying her.

Mary Bell was observed with great fascination by psychiatrists. As an eleven year-old double murderer - and female to boot - she was a rare specimen. Any hopes they might have had that she would open up to them were soon to be dashed. Mary Bell wasn't in the mood to talk. She also, so far at least, showed no sign of remorse or any understanding of the gravity of the crimes she had committed. Betty Bell was a frequent visitor to Red Bank. She brought gifts for Mary and seemed to be doing her best to keep her daughter's spirits up. On the outside though, Betty became quite infamous in tabloid circles for trying to sell the newspapers stories about Mary. The mothers of Martin Brown and Eileen Corrigan would not have been happy if they'd known the Bell family (or Betty Bell if you prefer) were trying to make money out of their daughter's criminal fame. Mary Bell was given permission in 1970 to visit Billy Bell - who was in prison in Preston. She enjoyed this visit as Billy Bell was one of the few people who could ever make her laugh.

This same year (1970), the now thirteen years-old Mary Bell accused a housemaster at Red Bank of sexually abusing her. Though the claim was investigated, Mary Bell's allegations were not believed by the authorities. It was judged that Mary Bell told so many different versions of the abuse allegation that the only possible conclusion to draw was that she had made it up. Her various descriptions of this abuse were at odds with one another and didn't form a consistent story. Many decades later there was an investigation into historic sex abuse at Red Bank and the investigation found there had been a problem at the centre going back many years. This later investigation made Mary Bell's 1970 claims seem more credible. At the time though no one was in much of a mood to believe Mary Bell about anything given that she'd recently lied through her teeth at a murder trial.

Mary Bell's parents went their separate ways around this time. They split up. Betty Bell appeared on television in 1972 for the show Midweek. Midweek was a BBC current affairs magazine show hosted by Ludovic Kennedy. Betty Bell was interviewed in a hotel. She look tired and glum, her blonde wig not fooling television viewers let alone the interviewer. Betty looked like a broken woman and couldn't even make eye contact with the interviewer as she gave brief responses in her soft Scottish accent. Betty was at a loss to explain why her daughter had become a killer at the age of eleven. Betty weakly suggested her arguments with Billy might have damaged Mary in some way. The Midweek show's piece on Mary Bell was framed around a strange allegation that she had posed for sexually suggestive photographs at Red Bank and shared pornographic material with other inmates. There wasn't much substance to either of these stories. Mary Bell had posed for a photograph in a minidress (which was a common fashion at the time) taken by her mother. The alleged pornography was a sex education book that was passed around between the inmates. It was all a storm in a teacup - especially compared to the sexual abuse allegations which everyone ignored a few years before.

The worrying headlines about Mary Bell prompted the local Labour MP Robert Brown to visit Red Bank. Mr Brown, presumably to assuage constituents, had made complaints about Mary Bell being housed in the area. He was permitted to meet Mary Bell and after this experience did a complete about turn and changed his mind. After the meeting, Mr Brown said that Mary Bell was intelligent and polite and seemed to be making very encouraging progress. It seems that Mary Bell wasn't at all what he expected. Robert Brown stopped complaining about Mary Bell being located in the area and praised Red Bank for the work they were doing. Another person who complained about Mary Bell was an MP named Fred Lee - who was Chancellor of the Duchy of Lancaster and 'Minister for the North'. Mr Lee said it was unrealistic to expect constituents to calmy accept Mary Bell in their area. Mr Lee was slapped down by the Labour government and told to go and visit Red Bank for himself just as Mr Brown had done. Political figures in Newcastle actually criticised Mr Lee for his comments and said as 'Minister for the North' he should be setting a better example and supporting places like Red Bank for the valuable work they do.

Mary Bell would spend four and a half years at Red Bank in

all. She got used to the place but it wasn't exactly paradise. Red Bank was quite bleak looking both inside and out. It looked like the derelict wing of a rundown secondary school from the outside and that aura was replicated inside. Red Bank could be quite claustrophobic with the little rooms but it did at least have some greenery and fresh air outside. When the place was closed down decades later, photographs of the inside showed constrictive corridors, murals on the wall, and a games room where inmates could play things like pool and table football. Institutions liked Red Bank had a vital function because they kept young offenders out of real prisons - where they would be at greater risk of harm, suicide, or simply getting lost in the system. Red Bank was designed to tailor itself to the needs of each specific inmate. There were school classes and also workshops to help boys learn a trade. It wasn't perfect but it was a lot better than sticking these offenders in a real prison.

Mary Bell had some tantrums at Red Bank and there were stories that she had sexual dalliances with some of the boys. On the whole though she made surprisingly good progress. Officials and politicians who met Mary Bell at Red Bank were surprised at how normal and likeable she was. They had heard all the stories about this 'Demon Child' with a heart of ice but the teenager they met at Red Bank was nothing like that at all. Mary Bell would say, many years later, that when she killed Brian Howe she was in a strange otherworldly haze of fury because she had just had an argument with her mother. So she took it out on Brian. Mary Bell claimed she had no idea what she was doing and never meant any harm to Martin and Brian. That was at odds with the evidence of Norma. Norma said that Mary Bell was perfectly lucid when she attacked Brian Howe. It would take a long time for Mary Bell to even admit she had killed those children. She never did this at Red Bank. Mary Bell seemed to have this defence mechanism where she felt if she didn't talk about her crimes or acknowledge they occurred then that meant they didn't actually happen.

Although she later blamed her mother for almost everything that happened in 1968, Betty Bell was fond of showing people letters Mary had sent her from Red Bank. The letters indicated that Mary Bell was close to her mother and needed her more than ever. Mary Bell was a young teenager locked up in a detention centre miles from home so the visits and support of her mother were vital. Betty Bell was still doing interviews with tabloids and trying to make money out of the criminal fame of her daughter. While the ethics of this were dubious, it was an easier way to make money than working as a prostitute in Glasgow. Betty seemed to be making the most of this limited spotlight - despite public utterances like her famous "Jesus was only nailed to the cross, I'm being hammered." She pretended it was hell being the mother of Mary Bell but in a strange way she seemed to be enjoying the attention. The staff at Red Bank didn't like Betty Bell very much. They thought she came across as an actor playing the part of a concerned mother. There was something insincere and shallow about Betty Bell to them. They must have wondered what life was like for Mary Bell when she lived with Betty in the 1960s.

Mary's apparently close bond with Betty was contradicted by a Home Office report on her progress. The report found that Mary Bell was making excellent progress and stated that a factor in this was Mary realising that her mother was not a good influence on her life. Mary Bell was judged by the report to be calm, friendly, and now capable of making rational decisions. The report recommended that Mary Bell could be released in 1975 - by which time she would be eighteen. This did not happen in the end and for good reason. The mothers of Martin Brown and Brian Howe would have been justifiably appalled if the extent of Mary Bell's punishment for shattering their lives and murdering their sons had been six years in a detention centre. June Richardson was so traumatised by the death of Martin that for a good while after the murder she would walk the streets looking for him. She refused to accept he was dead.

What had changed the most about Mary Bell in Red Bank was her ability to form friendships and also her ability to charm those who had to meet her. The little Mary Bell of 1968 lacked any of these qualities. The authorities didn't think that Mary Bell was a threat anymore. They deemed her aggression to be under control. In his report on Mary Bell before the 1968 trial, the physician David Westbury wrote, 'Mary's social techniques are primitive and take the form of automatic denial, ingratiation, manipulation, complaining, bullying, flight or violence.' Red Bank, along with a few years distance, seemed to have removed the worst parts of Mary Bell's character. Red Bank was run by a man named James Dixon who used to be in the Royal Navy. Mr Dixon was firm but fair and said to be a kind and trustworthy person. There is evidence that James Dixon became a surrogate father figure to Mary Bell and someone she looked up to. Mary Bell didn't want to leave Red Bank because it had become her home and she knew all the staff. When the time came to make that decision though the final say would rest with someone way above Mr Dixon's pay grade.

The strategy of Red Bank in their treatment of offenders was to focus on the present and the future and not dwell on the past. This was a big factor in why Mary Bell made good progress. She was able to put 1968 behind her and just live a day to day life. Not all of the staff there were in full agreement with this policy. Some believed that more effort should have been made to make Mary confront her crimes. Because this approach was avoided Mary was able to block them out and act as if they never happened. Mary Bell went through many counsellors at Red Bank but none of them got to know her very well or dug very deep into her character. Mary Bell regarded them with polite indifference. She was much more civilised and calm than the girl she was in 1968 but that didn't mean she was ready or willing to talk about her crimes or even own up to them. There is a theory that Mary Bell, noted as a cunning sort of character in 1968, manipulated the staff at Red Bank and played the role of reformed prisoner in the hope of an early release. The more credible explanation is that the passage of time and being taken out of Whitehouse Road tamed Mary Bell.

Reports on Mary Bell at Red Bank indicated that she had little memory of the events of 1968, including the trial. Whether she blanked this out or genuinely forgot most of it is hard to say. Mary Bell said the trial was simply a blur to her and she had no idea what was going on. She said she didn't even know that the group of men and women the QC's kept addressing in court where a jury and the people who had to decide her fate. The most surreal thing about Mary Bell is that she was unaware of the perception of her in the outside world. She didn't know she was famous and oblivious to the fact she was considered to be a monster. Mary Bell said this all came as a shock to her when she experienced freedom for the first time. Because she had blocked out her crimes and could barely remember 1968 it didn't occur to her that the society beyond detention centres and prisons remembered 1968 like it was yesterday and had followed her progress in the tabloids.

Society at large also hadn't forgotten the horrible and extraordinary crime case where two young girls were put on trial for murdering children and one of them was convicted.

Mary Bell would have been horrified to learn that her fame and notoriety wasn't confined to people who lived in Newcastle in the late 1960s. It applied to the entire country and the unenviable fame of Mary Bell would last for her entire life. Mary Bell would still be making national headlines as the 21st Century hovered into view. That is something the Mary

Bell of Red Bank wouldn't have been able to comprehend or believe. Mary Bell was so despised in the late 1960s and early 1970s that some people even compared her to Myra Hindley. Mary Bell really hated this comparison when she first heard about. She was horrified and amazed to learn that she was being compared to Myra Hindley of all people.

Myra Hindley was born in Manchester in 1942. She had a fairly bog standard background and became a clerk at an engineering firm when she left school. It was in 1961 that Hindley got a job as a typist at Millwards Merchandising and it was here that she met the vile and older Ian Brady. Brady loved reading Mein Kampf and seemed to be obsessed with Hitler. Hindley was completely besotted with Brady and he would regale her with tales of the Marquis de Sade and Nazis. Brady made Hindley die her hair blonde and start wearing leather clothes. He seemed to be trying to make her look like some 'Aryan' villain from Nazi Germany. Hindley even stopped going to church because Brady told her that God didn't exist. The couple were soon planning bank robberies together and it's a great pity they didn't stick to that plan. What they did instead was indescribably evil and constituted the most harrowing crimes anyone could imagine. Brady was a pompous weirdo with no moral compass and highly dangerous. He and Hindley became inseparable and the criminal career they forged together was evil beyond words. The first victim was teenager Pauline Reade. Hindley lured her to Saddleworth Moor while Brady followed on his motorbike. He then hit her with a shovel and fractured her skull. Brady raped Reade and slit her throat. Pauline's body was only discovered three decades later in 1987.

Twelve-year-old John Kilbride was the next victim. Brady raped him and cut his throat. Kilbride survived having his throat cut and was then strangled by Brady. It was Hindley who had been the bait in the couple luring Kilbride to the moor. In 1964, twelve year-old Keith Bennett and ten-year-old

Lesley Ann Downey were murdered by Brady and Hindley. Keith was lured into a car by Hindley and she took him to the moor where Brady raped and murdered him. Keith's body, much to the distress of his mother (who later became friends with June Richardson when they campaigned together for the rights of the famalies affected by violent crime), was never found. Ten-year-old Lesley Ann Downey was abducted and taken to Hindley's house where she was tortured and then raped and strangled. Brady and Hindley recorded a sixteen minute tape of Lesley pleading for her life and screaming. The last victim was seventeen year-old Edward Evans, who Brady killed with an axe in an attempt to impress David Smith - the husband of Hindley's sister. Brady, who was completely insane, had always boasted of his murderous exploits and wanted to prove he hadn't made them up.

Smith called the police and the ghastly crimes of Brady and Hindley began to be uncovered. Ian Brady was described as arrogant and aloof at his trial. He tried to pin the blame on David Smith - which was desperate and doomed to failure. Brady showed no emotion when the awful tape of Lesley Ann Downey's screams were heard. He was found guilty and sentenced to life in prison. Capital punishment had only recently been abolished so Brady had a close shave when it came to avoiding a death sentence. Most people at the time probably would have been delighted to see Ian Brady hung for his crimes. The Moors Murders were incredibly harrowing and upsetting for the general public at the time. You could say that society was less innocent in the 1960s. Crimes like this were simply far less reported and less prevalent too. The thought that a woman too was involved in the torture and murder of children was beyond belief to society at the time.

Myra Hindley pretended she played no role in the murders and rapes in court but Brady, who wasn't half as clever as he thought he was, unwittingly implicated Hindley when he told the court that after the assault on Lesley Ann Downey they had all put their clothes back on. This implied that Hindley had been a very active participant in the abuse.

Like his fellow Scottish lunatic Dennis Nilsen, Ian Brady was an insufferable pseudo-intellectual bore in prison and wrote endless letters, essays, and books. Brady, like Nilsen, also endlessly complained about his treatment and the standard of prisons. He even went on a hunger strike at one point and had to be force fed. It's fair to say that few people had any sympathy for him. Most people probably hoped he was having an awful time. When, towards the end of her life, Myra Hindley seemed to have a vague possibly of release, Ian Brady was much put out by this and kicked up a fuss. He said Hindley always downplayed her part in the murders and blamed everything on him. Myra Hindley would later blame Brady for the murders and said that she was fearful of him and was abused.

In cases like this it is fairly common for the female half of the killer duo to claim after capture that they were a victim too and had no choice. "I had this obsession about him," said Hindley of Brady. "This infatuation, I believed it to be love. I think it stemmed from the fact Brady was so different to anyone I had met. He seemed cloaked in an aura of mystery I could never quite penetrate, never quite solve and this unknowability intrigued me and continued to enhance his attraction to me." Despite her expressions of remorse and attempts to get parole, no one really believed that Hindley was innocent and she will probably forever be the most infamous female figure in British true crime history. There were attempts, especially by Lord Longford, to release Myra Hindley from prison but the newspapers and public were appalled by this. Hindley died in prison in 2002. Myra Hindley was still so despised that when she died the prison authorities struggled to find an undertaker willing to handle the cremation.

Although they had both been responsible for the deaths of

children and both provoked great public anger there was a big difference between Mary Bell and Hindley. The public were against Hindley ever being released but the great majority of the public were in favour of Mary Bell being released so long as she served a reasonable length of time in incarceration and also proved that she was rehabilitated. This would mean that Mary Bell had to reach a point where she was no danger to anyone and sorry for what she had done in 1968. The general view was that Mary Bell, so long as she changed, should not have to spend the rest of her life being punished for the things an eleven year-old girl did in 1968 because Mary Bell was longer that eleven year-old girl. During her time at Red Bank, the anger and fury inside Mary Bell seemed to melt away. She was no longer a threat to society but it was more difficult to say if she was sorry for her crimes or had experienced any guilt or regret because that was a subject she still refused to be drawn on.

BLACKPOOL

While she was at Red Bank, Mary Bell passed her CSE in English. Everyone at the centre was quite proud of how Mary Bell was turning out. However, to the fury of Mr Dixon and Red Bank, and the horror of Mary Bell, the Home Office decided in November 1973 that Mary Bell would be transferred to HM Prison Styal in Cheshire. Styal was founded as an orphanage, but became a prison for women in 1962. Mary Bell was given no advance warning about the transfer. One day she was simply told to pack her belongings and get ready to leave. Red Bank were not given any warning about this either and they were furious. They considered it to be a very stupid decision to send Mary Bell to a prison when she was making such good progress at Red Bank. From high above HM Prison Styal looked like a series of cottages in the middle of fields. It actually looked pleasant from a distance. At ground level though and inside it had the bleakness you'd associate with such a place and wasn't an especially nice environment.

Red Bank had become Mary Bell's home. It was all she had known since early 1969. She had her own room and friends there. The staff were familiar to her. She liked Mr Dixon. To be unexpectedly wrenched from Red Bank and dropped into a female prison with complete strangers was a terrifying and discombobulating experience for Mary Bell. The Home Office told the press that Mary Bell was moved from Red Bank because she was now 'maturing' and as a teenage girl nearing womanhood it was not suitable for her to be the lone girl at Red Bank among boys anymore. Therefore the decision had been made to move her to a closed prison for women. The Home Office said it was a choice between Holloway and Styal and Styal was chosen because of its cottage system and better facilities for young inmates.

Betty Bell told the media that Mary was at her 'wit's end' at Styal and all the good work by Red Bank was at risk of being undone. Betty Bell lodged a complaint about the transfer with the Labour MP George Grant - who promised to look into the matter and see what could be done. In truth though there wasn't much Mr Grant could do. James Dixon, the headmaster of Red Bank, made regular visits to Styal to talk to Mary Bell. Mr Dixon told the newspapers that Styal was not a suitable place for Mary Bell and she missed her friends at Red Bank. He said he would in no way want to minimise how serious and awful her crimes were but Mary had changed and was no longer that feral little girl in Scotswood. Mr Dixon said he was worried about Mary Bell's future because all the work done by Red Bank was now at risk. He told the press that what Mary Bell needed more than anything was hope. She had to believe she had a future.

Mr Dixon said that Mary Bell now acknowledged her crimes

and was aware of what she had done. Betty Bell and James Dixon both told the press that they had seen a marked deterioration in Mary Bell since her transfer to HM Prison Styal. She was more withdrawn, depressed, and didn't look very well. Mary Bell was at HM Prison Styal from 1973 to 1976. She seemed to go through different experimental phases while in the prison. Mary pretended she was a man and had some prison affairs with other women. Because she was still so young she didn't attract any violence and by all accounts brought out the maternal side of some of the other inmates. This seems strange to us today because we assume that those who commit crimes against children are the most despised and at risk of anyone in a prison. For whatever reason Mary Bell was not a target when she entered the prison system. Maybe it would have been very different if Mary had committed those crimes when she was an adult. Mary's infamy didn't really cut much ice at Styal. She was seen as a confused teenager who did something bad when she was a little kid.

Betty Bell was a regular visitor to Mary in prison. She noted that Mary seemed to be more closed off and quiet than she was at Red Bank. It is said that Billy Bell did not visit Mary because he had a morbid fear of prisons. Mary did correspond with him though. Mary Bell had appeals for parole denied while at Styal. In 1976, Mary Bell was moved to Moor Court open prison in Stoke-on-Trent, Staffordshire. She was now nineteen years old. Moor Court was a beautiful country mansion in lovely surroundings. The house was constructed by businessman Alfred Bolton in 1890. There were fifty rooms and a number of annexes. A country house in Jacobean style, Moor Court was built in stone with tiled roofs and shaped gables. It was certainly a far cry from Whitehouse Road. Moor Court was acquired by the Home Office in 1962 and turned into a correctional centre and open prison. Years later, in 1989, Moor Court was purchased by the famous masked wrestler Kendo Nagasaki. Kendo Nagasaki (real name Peter Thornley) has used Moor Court to teach courses in zen meditation. It's hard to say who the most famous resident has been in Moor Court's long history but chances are it's a tossup between Mary Bell and Kendo.

An open prison is a place with minimal supervision and security. The prisoners are deemed to be no risk and as such are free to potter around and are not locked in a cell. Those in an open prison are encouraged to take work placements to help them prepare for life on the outside. Mary Bell was on a secretarial course at Moor Court. She was close to release - which made what she did next curious. The only explanation is that Mary Bell did not want to be released and wanted a longer stay at Moor Court. In 1977 the twenty year-old Mary Bell escaped with a fellow prisoner named Annette Priest. They simply climbed over the wall and wandered off. Annette Priest was a twenty-one year-old prostitute who had been sent to prison for stealing money from her 'punters'. She was evidently Mary Bell's best friend at Moor Court. When the media got wind of the fact that Mary Bell had escaped from prison it made headlines in the papers. The police tried to dampen down the bubbling hysteria and said Mary Bell was not dangerous. She was a rehabilitated young woman of twenty who was due for release. The police said this was a missing persons case and not an escaped lunatic on the run.

It was reported that Mary Bell and Priest were seen thumbing a lift in Cheshire but their whereabouts were unknown. The police in Staffordshire alerted their police colleagues in Northumberland and Yorkshire (where Annette Priest was from) to be on watch in case either of the two young women tried to make their way home to relatives. It turned out though that Mary Bell and Annette Priest had picked up a lift from a petty thief named Clive Shirtcliffe (in his late twenties) and his friend Keith Hibbert (who was in his early thirties). You don't get names like that anymore do you?

They sound like characters from a Carry On film. Shirtcliffe and Hibbert didn't have the faintest idea at first that they'd just picked up the infamous Mary Bell. In those days it wasn't unusual for young women to hitchhike and jump in the car of a complete stranger. That wouldn't happen so much today.

Mary Bell told the two men that they'd escaped from an open prison. Mary added that she'd been locked up for ten years. This didn't make any sense to Shirtcliffe because Mary Bell looked like a teenager. How could she have been banged up for ten years? Then the penny dropped. He realised who she was. He had the infamous Tyneside Strangler in his car.

Shirtcliffe and Hibbert decided to head for Blackpool. There were a number of firsts for Mary Bell on this jaunt to the seaside. She had never been to a nightclub, she had never got drunk, never been in a restaurant, and she had never been to a funfair. Mary Bell did all of these things in Blackpool. It felt a lot like she was using this illicit trip trying to make up for missing out on her normal teenage years. Because she wasn't used to alcohol it didn't take much at all to get Mary Bell drunk. Mary Bell was finally able to do some of the things that teenagers take for granted. Mary loved the lights and music of the funfair and went on the big dipper. It was all a novelty to her.

Clive Shirtcliffe said he didn't dream of turning Mary Bell in to the authorities because he'd been in prison himself and had sympathy for the two escapees. The four of them booked into a seafront boarding house and Shirtcliffe, if his claims are true, took Mary Bell's virginity that night. Shirtcliffe and Hibbert later told the media that Mary Bell disputed the events of 1968. She told them she wasn't evil and insisted that it was Norma who killed Brian Howe. Mary Bell also told the two men that she didn't mean to harm Martin Brown and it was an accident which occurred during a fight. None of this was very believable and indicated that Mary, contrary to what James Dixon told the newspapers, still hadn't faced up to her crimes. Martin Brown was four years old so the idea that he was in a fight with a scrappy girl seven years his senior did strain credibility.

The next morning the newspapers were full of stories about Mary Bell being on the run. Keith Hibbert said that Mary was shocked to discover that she was famous and considered to be one of the most evil people in recent history. Hibbert said that Mary Bell was especially hurt to learn that she was often compared to Myra Hindley. Mary was put in a kiss me quick hat by way of disguise and they all departed Blackpool to head south. On the way they stopped at a hairdressers and Mary Bell got her hair cut short so she wouldn't be recognised. Clive Shirtcliffe said the disguise worked because they actually passed through a police roadblock which was designed to capture Mary Bell. One person who was astonished by the news headlines was June Richardson - the mother of Martin Brown. Mary Bell was a name that June, happily, had managed to avoid for a good few years but now Mary Bell was suddenly splashed all over the newspapers again.

June took the paranoid step of taking her children out of school and watching over them like a bodyguard. She didn't want to take any chances though of course they were in no real danger. Mary Bell wasn't going to make her way to Newcastle and start murdering June's remaining children. Mary Bell was no longer a threat to anyone. June knew that she wasn't thinking straight and over reacting but just seeing the name Mary Bell in the newspapers brought everything flooding back and threw her into a panic. June said she was angered that the police didn't tell her about Mary Bell's escape and she had to read about it in the newspapers. You can understand June's raw emotions but the police knew no one was in danger from Mary Bell (now a meek and mild twenty year-old woman and not a feral violent eleven year-old) and saw no need to alarm anyone - least of all June.

Maybe they could have phoned or visited her though just to explain that.

Clive Shirtcliffe drove down the M6 to Derby and the gang (minus one) stayed on a canal boat. Annette Priest had parted company with the gang by now. She decided to head for her home city Leeds. The newspaper headline were all about Mary Bell and not Priest so she had easier time not being noticed. The remaining three went out to a club drinking and gave Mary Bell the fake name 'Robinson' after listening to Simon and Garfunkel on a jukebox. So they decided if anyone inquired what Mary's name was they would say Mary Robinson. Shirtcliffe spent the night with Mary on the boat. He said he saw no sign or evil or malice in her. At this point Clive Shirtcliffe had run out of money - which is not surprising given how many drinks he must have purchased for the two penniless escapees. Shirtcliffe decided to go to his mother's house and pretend that Mary was his girlfriend.

Mary Bell had dyed her hair so Shirtcliffe's mother did not recognise this famous fugitive. Mrs Shirtcliffe allowed Mary to stay in her son's room but he was told to sleep downstairs because she didn't want any hanky panky in the house. Clive Shirtcliffe simply waited until his mother was asleep and then crept upstairs to spend the night with Mary. What with this and the canal boat capers, Clive Shirtcliffe sounded like Robin Askwith in a 1970s comedy film. The next morning Mary Bell was rumbled at last after three days on the run. She was arrested while in a car with Shirtcliffe and Hibbert. The newspaper reports indicated that the car was parked near a house connected to a woman named Susan moore - who Mary had become friends with at Styal. It appears that Mary Bell was trying to make contact with Moore (Susan Moore cashed in on her Mary Bell link by selling a story to the tabloids and claiming she had taught Mary about sex).

Mary Bell's ultimate objective was apparently to go to London and get a job. This seems odd because she was due to be released and fixed up with a job anyway. It appears that Mary Bell had some sort of fantasy of creating a new identity for herself and going it alone. This was never destined to be anything more than a fantasy because she would have been recognised sooner or later. And how was she supposed to stay in touch with her mother? Did she even want to stay in touch with Betty? Clive Shirtcliffe said Mary Bell was calm when she saw the police cars and thanked him for everything before departing back into custody. He never saw her again despite writing letters. She either never got these letters or ignored them. Maybe the prison system decided not to pass them on. Clive Shirtcliffe claimed that Mary Bell wanted him to her pregnant but this didn't happen. Mary Bell was taken to Risely Remand Centre in Warrington after her arrest.

Clive Shirtcliffe was misty eyed and nostalgic about his three days with Mary Bell for the rest of his life (obituary notices for the Derby Telegraph indicate that Shirtcliffe died in 2020 at the age of 71). Clive Shirtcliffe described the Mary Bell of 1977 as a sleeping princess who had finally woken up. June Richardson and Eileen Corrigan probably would have described Mary Bell as more of a sleeping nightmare suddenly awoken rather than a sleeping princess. Clive Shirtcliffe and Keith Hibbert had to appear at Derby Magistrates Court for sheltering Mary Bell and Annette Priest. Each of them was given a six month sentence suspended for two years and fined £100. If his interviews were anything to go by, Shirtcliffe must have considered that a small price to pay for a few nights with Mary Bell. The barrister defending them said Clive Shirtcliffe and Keith Hibbert sheltered Mary Bell because she wasn't being treated very well by the prison system (a ridiculous defence because she was at Moor Court open prison - which was like a beautiful country mansion) and had consulted a social worker on what to about her - whereupon they were arrested. By that time though Mary Bell and Annette Priest were gone anyway. Annette Priest was arrested in Leeds a few days after Mary Bell was back in custody.

Mary Bell's punishment for escaping was a loss of prison privileges for 28 days. In 1978 she was moved to HM Prison Askham Grange in North Yorkshire. This was another open prison. While at the prison Mary did a secretarial course at college (under a different name) and also had work experience as a waitress in York (for which she earned £5 a week after deductions for her bus fare). Despite the fact she was still technically in prison, Mary Bell seemed to have a surprisingly active sex life around this time by all accounts. She later claimed to have got pregnant and had an abortion while at Askham. The father was, according to Mary, a 'respectable' married man. Another man, who kept his identity secret and was only identified as 'Alan', told one of the tabloids many years later that he had a romance with Mary Bell while she was at Askham. It maybe wasn't that surprising that Mary Bell had an active love life at this time because she was in an open prison and encouraged to mix in the community to get used to life on the outside.

Alan told a newspaper in 1998 that he fell in love with Mary Bell but the authorities stopped the affair because he had a criminal record and worried he might be a bad influence on her. Alan, who was 27 when he met Mary Bell, said that Mary told him him about losing her virginity in Blackpool but said she'd only slept with Clive Shirtcliffe because she feared she might have to sleep with both him and Keith Hibbert if she didn't pick one. You suspect Clive Shirtcliffe would have been very hurt by this revelation and probably disputed it. Anyway, Alan described Mary Bell as 'bubbly' and kind. He did not try to make her talk about 1968 and she rarely brought up the subject herself. He did say though that Mary Bell told him she ended up in prison for having a fight. In her own mind, Mary Bell had apparently created this false memory where Martin Brown was killed in an accident after they had a scrap and then Norma killed Brian Howe.

Alan said that Mary Bell had a mild obsession with Myra Hindley and was quick to say she would have attacked Hindley if she'd ended up in the same prison. Being compared to Myra Hindley was a particular sore point for Mary Bell. Alan told the press that he would have married Mary Bell and believed she was innocent but he never tried to contact her again after being warned off by the authorities because he knew it might effect her parole. Alan said the only time he saw 'evil' in Mary Bell's eyes was when they were in bed together one night. With this mind it is rather odd that he wanted to marry her. Alan's mother chipped in with a few comments about Mary Bell and none of them were nice. She described Mary Bell as false and chippy and said she couldn't wait to see the back of her.

Back at Askham Grange there were actually prisoners there with babies and Mary Bell would sometimes help out with looking after them. A woman named Marjorie Spragg became friends with Mary Bell at Askham and said Mary would look after her infant daughter Kelly. Ms Spragg said Mary bell was kind and trustworthy and she didn't worry about Mary's awful criminal past because that happened a long time ago. Mary Bell wanted to work with children for a career. Though she was still not confessional about her crimes this ambition suggested she wanted to try and make amends in some way. Mary Bell later said there were a lot of drugs at Askham but she never touched them. She did though use drugs when she was released. There were a number of stories about Mary Bell in the newspapers as she neared her release. There were stories that she had lucrative offers from magazines to tell her story, One newspaper claimed a social worker believed she might become a fashion model.

It was said too that Mary wanted to go back home to Newcastle when she was released - though the authorities were unlikely to allow this to happen. Later on though there were tales of Mary Bell being seen in pubs on Tyneside and even living there for a time. The most common and (realistic) theme in the press clippings about Mary Bell was that it was going to be very difficult for her to live a normal life on the outside. In May, 1980, the twenty-three year-old Mary Bell was finally released. She was given a new name to protect her real identity. Mary Bell was not too thrilled to be leaving prison. She was terrified. Mary would have happily just stayed at Moor Court or Askham for the rest of her life. In those places she had a bed, no rent or bills to pay, free meals, and nice surroundings. Now she would have to fend for herself. This was a frightening prospect for a twenty-three year-old woman who had been locked up since 1968.

FROZEN

It was a very different world Mary Bell entered in 1980 compared to the one she'd left in 1968 but she had of course already had a small taste of this new world. Britain now had its first female prime minister, the hottest band was Blondie and the biggest film was The Empire Strikes Back. A lot of the current news headlines revolved around the hunt for a terrifying serial killer who had become known as the Yorkshire Ripper. Mary Bell was a bit like the character Austin Powers, frozen in the 1960s and now thrown into a modern world that was largely alien to her. Who knows where Mary Bell would have been in 1983 if she hadn't killed those two boys. Perhaps she would have been working as a waitress alongside Norma in Newcastle. The release of Mary Bell did not go unnoticed by the tabloids and the hunt was on as far as they were concerned to see who could get the first photograph of this infamous young woman. Mary stayed with her probation officer for a few weeks when she left prison. It was with great reluctance that she left this house. There is evidence that Mary was fixed up with a factory job in

Yorkshire for a time. Perhaps she tried to hook up with Annette Priest while she was there?

There wasn't much that Mary Bell liked about freedom. She was used to living in institutions and having everything done for her. Life on the outside was considerably more complex and frightening. "She wishes to be given a chance to live a normal life and to be left alone," said the Home Office about her release. The subtext of that comment was directed squarely at the tabloids. Despite all the stories about Mary Bell selling her story for money (which she knew only too well would have invited unwanted resentment and controversy) or becoming a model (this latter speculation was plainly unrealistic), none of this transpired and she has lived a fairly impoverished life since leaving prison. Jobs and money were hard to come by and so Mary Bell, like most of us, had to duck and dive and eke out a modest living. Mary Bell reconnected with her mother after prison and there is evidence that they lived together for a period. There must have been times post prison where Betty was all Mary had left in the world. She was a complete stranger to her siblings and never managed to become a part of their lives again.

Though the Newcastle of her childhood could be a harsh place for the working classes and Mary had known real poverty in the 1960s, she was always a loyal Geordie at heart and missed the North East. The family of Martin Brown complained, some years later, that Mary Bell was seen drinking in pubs on Tyneside and went back there a lot. A stipulation in her release was that she was supposed to stay away from Newcastle (where the relatives of her victims still mostly lived) and that general area but at some point she either flouted this instruction or it was pared down as a condition. Because she has lived out of the spotlight under an assumed name we don't know all the details about Mary Bell's life in the 1980s but we know a lot more about her than Norma.

We know that Mary Bell went to university (which one we don't know) but dropped out because she decided it wasn't her cup of tea. If you are a nervous freshly released con with a horrific secret in your past and an assumed identity then a campus full of hundreds of people is probably not the most comfortable environment to be in. Mary Bell just wanted to be left alone. Crowds of people were her worst nightmare. Mary Bell lived a very threadbare bedsit sort of life in the immediate years after prison. She went through a period where she used drugs and also stole from some shops. The thought of being sent back to prison didn't hold much fear for Mary Bell. She would have welcomed it in those days. Her release didn't create much controversy because 1968 was a long time ago and she was a child when she committed those crimes. Most felt that eleven years in prison or institutions was a fair punishment.

There were some dissenting voices - mostly from those on the right. A few Conservatives MPs, after Mary Bell escaped from Moor Court, wanted to know why she was in an open prison and why she was due for release. They wanted Mary Bell locked up forever and portrayed her as a dangerous lunatic who could never change. Mary Bell probably saw some of this commentary in newspapers. Although she was a completely different person from the little girl who roamed around Scotswood with Norma there was no escaping from 1968. Mary Bell was still having to pay a heavy price for the terrible things she did when she was eleven years-old. The tabloids got their prized photograph of Mary Bell quite soon after her release. One of them got a snap of her walking down a street with a long strapped handbag. She was wearing jeans and a tight top. Mary Bell had a neck length mop of hair which wasn't very flattering and made her look older than her twenty-three years. She didn't much resemble the angelic little girl in that famous 1960s photograph. The large sunglasses indicated a desire not to be recognised.

It was irresponsible of the tabloids to put a current picture of Mary Bell in the newspapers because she lived under an assumed name for her own safety. The view of the tabloids, or some of them at any rate, was that this was a convicted child killer who didn't deserve any special consideration or respect. In the years to come Mary Bell would have to go to courts to protect her privacy. Mary Bell must have cursed the eleven year-old version of herself. That eleven year-old girl ruined her entire life and yet at the time was completely oblivious to this. The 1968 version of Mary Bell presumed she could talk her way out of trouble and then go home to her dog. All these years later Mary Bell had learned the hard way that the girl she was in 1968 wasn't very bright and wasn't very nice.

Mary Bell seemed to move around a lot in the early 1980s. There were stories she was living in Suffolk. Tabloid photographs of her suddenly stopped because the newspapers were warned off by the authorities. The authorities wanted to put a blackout around Mary Bell and have everyone forgot about her. Mary Bell would have loved this to happen but in the end it didn't. Whatever she did she couldn't run away from her past. It always seemed to catch up with her in the end. There aren't too many true crime parallels with Mary Bell of people going to prison at a tender age for murder and then being rehabilitated but one such case sometimes mentioned is that of Jasmine Richardson. Jasmine Richardson is one of the youngest serial killers in history. In Alberta, Canada, in 2006, she helped murder her parents and stabbed her eight year-old brother to death. She was just twelve years-old at the time. Jasmine Richardson was heavily under the influence of her twenty-three year-old boyfriend Jeremy Steinke - a nutty character who claimed to be a werewolf.

The motive for the murders was that Richardson was distraught and upset that her family didn't approve of her relationship with Steinke. Of course they didn't approve of the relationship. She was only twelve! Steinke was naturally deemed to be involved in the murders.

This diabolical pair had met through online vampire chat forums. Steinke had proposed marriage to Richardson and she accepted. When her parents (predictably) disapproved she decided to be a full accomplice in the murder of her entire immediate family. Jasmine apparently pretended to be fifteen years-old when she met Jeremy Steinke and while that's slightly better than being twelve it didn't make things markedly different. Steinke was still consorting with what he knew must be an underage girl. Just before the murders the pair had apparently watched the Oliver Stone film Natural Born Killers and drawn inspiration from the serial killer movie. Steinke, with Jasmine Richardson's help, stabbed her parents and then Jasmine Richardson stabbed her young brother Jacob in the chest. Steinke then slit Jacob's throat. Jacob had begged for his life but they still killed him. Jasmine Richardson said she killed her brother because she felt it would be cruel to let him grow up with no parents (as we saw in the Killer Kids chapter, this was the same twisted rationale Kim Edwards used for murdering her sister).

A few hours after these brutal and callous murders, Steinke and Jasmine Richardson were seen laughing and joking together in a diner. Jasmine Richardson said she helped kill her family because she thought it would bring her closer to Steinke. She was clearly mentally ill and highly disturbed. It obviously didn't take Miss Marple to deduce that Steinke and Jasmine Richardson were responsible for these murders. They were in custody fairly soon. Jasmine Richardson and Jeremy Steinke were both convicted for their crimes. Steinke received three life sentences but Jasmine Richardson, in a move that angered many Canadians, was released after ten years and given a new identity. Because of her age, Jasmine Richardson could be only be convicted of ten years in prison under Canadian law. Jasmine Richardson took a university course near the end of her sentence and was judged by the authorities to have genuine remorse and regret for her crimes. While that may or may not be true it obviously isn't much consolation to the three dead members of her family.

Jeremy Steinke, naturally, got a much harsher sentence. They basically locked Steinke up and threw the key away - which doesn't seem unreasonable given the circumstances. He is clearly a highly dangerous and manipulative man. Steinke's friend Kacy Lancaster, who was nineteen at the time of the murders, was charged with being an accessory for driving them away from the scene and helping to remove evidence. She was eventually given a sentence of one year under house arrest. Jasmine Richardson was released in 2016 and now has her identity protected. The authorities believe she has been completely rehabilitated. You can't help feeling that Jasmine Richardson got a light sentence not simply because of her age but also because of her gender. It hardly seems fair that young Jacob lost his life in brutal fashion yet his sister is now a free woman with most of her life still ahead of her. Whatever happens to Jasmine Richardson now will never erase her infamy. She seems destined to remain Canada's youngest multiple killer for a very long time.

Another young killer who changed was Ruth Cooper. On May 14, 1985, 78 year-old Ruth Pelke of Gary, Indiana, had a visit from four local girls who claimed to be interested in arranging some Bible lessons. The girls were Denise Thomas, aged 14, Karen Corder, aged 16, April Beverly, aged 15, and lastly - but by no means least - fifteen year-old Ruth Cooper. Cooper was the dominant personality in this little gang. She was the ringleader. The girls bunked off school that day and had drunk alcohol and smoked pot. You probably won't be surprised to learn that it wasn't really Bible lessons that had drawn them to the home of Ruth Pelke. The girls were there to see if the old lady had anything worth stealing. At some point things quickly got out of hand. Pelke was struck with a vase and then Ruth Cooper stabbed her to death. "Where's the money, bitch?" Cooper had demanded. The knife wounds were mostly to the chest. In all, Ruth Cooper stabbed Ruth Pelke over 30 times.

These heartless girls then ransacked the house looking for valuables. Their paltry reward for this vile crime was a mere $10. They did though find Pelke's car keys and so took her car - not that was worth any money. As you might imagine, a bunch of schoolgirls driving around in their victim's car were not exactly difficult to catch and these vile young criminals were soon in custody. The other three girls got lengthy prison sentences of varying degrees. Ruth Cooper though, as the ACTUAL killer, got the death penalty. Given her tender age this was a controversial decision. Cooper's defence team had argued that she was a damaged child who had been shuttled around various schools and suffered from abuse and neglect at home. They believed that she could be rehabilitated. The prosecution though argued that a girl capable of stabbing to death a kind old lady could never be rehabilitated and was a lost cause. There was a lot of anger in the local community over this heartless murder and the prosecution tapped into that aura.

There was a palpable desire to see some sort of vengeance extracted for what had happened to Ruth Pelke. Not everyone agreed with this approach though. The concept of giving someone the death penalty for a crime committed when they were fifteen was divisive to say the least. Ruth Cooper was violent and troubled in custody and lived up to her billing as one of the most cold hearted and dangerous kids in America. Her new residence was eventually on Death Row at the Indiana Women's Prison. In 1987, the Indiana legislature passed a bill moving the minimum age for a defendant in a death penalty case from ten years old to sixteen years old. This was clearly a reaction to the Paula Cooper case though - at this time - Cooper's status wasn't affected. There was though a concerted campaign to get Paula Cooper off Death

Row and this campaign was supported by Pope John Paul II. In the end all the pressure paid off. In 1988, after a Supreme Court decision, the death penalty was banned for defendants under the age of sixteen at the time of the crime. The authorities in Indiana took Paula Cooper off Death Row in 1989 and her sentence was reduced to life in prison.

It seems that, against all the odds, Paula Cooper did change in the end. She gained a number of educational qualifications in prison and became a tutor to other inmates. One of the most remarkable developments in this case that the fact that Ruth Pelke's grandson Bill forgave Paula Cooper and even campaigned to get her off Death Row. Bill, who was a Vietnam veteran, said he was initially furious at Cooper and wanted her to die but he came to realise this is not what his deeply religious grandmother would have wanted. Bill even met Paula in person and even, you might say, became friends with her. Paula Cooper was released from prison in 2013. She was 43 years-old and a long way removed from the feral drunken fifteen year-old kid who had killed Ruth Pelke. Life on the outside was not easy for Paula Cooper though. She had spent her entire adult life in prison and found it difficult to cope out in the 'real world'. In 2015 she committed suicide by shooting herself in the head. If she had really changed - and all the evidence suggests that she HAD - then Paula Cooper would have had to live with the knowledge and guilt of what she had done in 1985. That was a burden that no one would wish for.

It is not easy to compare Mary Bell to other killers who committed their crimes when they were very young. All crimes have different details and motivations. Jasmine Richardson killed to be with her boyfriend (as did the British teen criminal Kim Edwards) whereas Paula Cooper was a financially motivated killer. These motivations did not apply to Mary Bell when she murdered two children in 1968. The question of why Mary Bell killed those two children was never answered. The psychiatrists who studied Mary Bell after her arrest said these were crimes with no motive. The closest Mary Bell came to an explanation was blaming her mother. She said she was in a foul mood after an argument with her mother when Brian Howe died. Mary also accused her mother of allowing men to sexually abuse her. Even if we took these claims as truth (and not everyone believes that Mary Bell was telling the truth about the sexual abuse) they still don't explain why she murdered two boys. There are, tragically, many victims of sexual abuse but they don't murder other children as a way to cope or let off steam. So why did Mary Bell kill? Was she just born evil?

Those who believe that people are born evil point to the presence of certain innate traits or characteristics that may predispose someone to engage in malevolent actions. Genetics, brain structure, and personality traits are some of the factors that are often cited as evidence of a biological basis for evil behaviour. Studies have shown that certain genetic variations can be associated with traits such as impulsivity, aggression, or psychopathy, which are commonly linked to antisocial or harmful actions. On the other hand, proponents of the belief that people are shaped by experience would point out the powerful influence of environmental factors on human development. From early childhood experiences to societal influences, the environment in which people grow and mature can play a significant role in shaping their moral compass and ethical decision-making. Traumatic events, exposure to violence, or lack of positive role models can all contribute to the development of behaviour that society may deem as "evil."

People are complex and multifaceted, with multiple factors interacting to influence individual actions and choices. While some people may possess genetic predispositions or inherent personality traits that make them more susceptible to engaging in harmful behaviour, the role of environmental influences cannot be ignored. A person's upbringing, cultural background, socioeconomic status, and life experiences all contribute to the formation of their moral beliefs and values. We can probably say right off the bat that Mary Bell lacked positive role models. Her father was a criminal and her mother was a prostitute. Both of Mary Bell's parents drank too much. One of the men ('Alan') who had a fling with Mary Bell in the late 1970s said she told him that when she was a little girl she sometimes slept in a tent in the garden to avoid her mother's temper and the arguments Betty had with Billy. Mary Bell experienced poverty and a lot of abuse by her mother when she was very young. There were the overdoses caused by Betty leaving pills around and also Betty trying to give Mary away and leaving her with relatives and friends. Abandonment issues can lead to emotional volatility.

There is a lot in Mary Bell's childhood which was bad and damaging but deciphering why someone so young becomes a killer is not easy. You can't just blame social services or say the mother was terrible (although the mother WAS terrible). Mary Bell's case was so unusual as to be practically unique in Britain for a time. If you blame bad childhoods for young killers it becomes complex because you can count the killers as young as Mary in Britain's history on one hand. There are hundreds of millions of people who had a bad childhood in Britain's history but only a handful of them ever killed children when they were still children themselves. How bad was Mary Bell's childhood compared to other really bad childhoods? It all depends on whether you believe Mary Bell's later claims that her mother press ganged her into prostitution at the age of four. You can't really explain Mary Bell either by saying she was born evil as if she was some supernatural horror villain. There must have been more to it than that.

There are certainly theories that Mary Bell experienced some sort of head trauma in her childhood and this, along with all the other bad aspects to her upbringing, created a child who couldn't distinguish between right and wrong and fantasy (or 'fancy' as her QC put it) and reality. Mary Bell could never explain why she killed two children. All she could say was that she went into a strange fog and didn't mean them any harm. She did at least come to accept she did those things in the end - after years of deflection and blaming her mother and Norma. This meant she had to cope with years of guilt and regret. No one in 1968 thought she had the ability to feel emotions like this but the rehabilitated Mary Bell could. Her early years out of prison were difficult. She was moved around and felt as if she didn't belong anywhere. Mary Bell was also terrified of media intrusion and neighbours finding out who she really was. She couldn't see many reasons to go on but in 1984 she would find what she was looking for. A purpose in life and a reason to get up in the morning. In 1984, Mary Bell, forever doomed to be called names like the Tyneside Strangler and Demon Child in crime related articles, became a mother.

WE FIND MARY BELL!

On the 25th of May 1984, Mary Bell gave birth to a daughter. The father was a man named Stephen O'Brien - who she was now living with. Due to Mary Bell's criminal background and fairly recent release from prison, Mary Bell's daughter was a ward of court on the application of the local authority. Mary and O'Brien were allowed to keep the child with a supervision order. The tabloid rag the News of the World got wind of this development and reported it. This was a decision bereft of ethics because Mary Bell's daughter had nothing to do with the events of 1968. She had no control over who her mother happened to be. Mary Bell's daughter wasn't going to have a normal life if all of this was splashed around in the newspapers. Mary Bell therefore took legal action and obtained an injunction which prevented the media reporting any details about her daughter until she was eighteen. It has been alleged that Mary Bell went by the name Helen Foster when she got out of prison but this (even if true) had to be changed more than once. It must have been confusing for Mary Bell's daughter but she still grew up oblivious to what her mother had done in the past. Mary Bell only told her daughter about 1968 when she had no choice some years later.

In 1987, Mary Bell might have noted with some interest a BBC Screen Two drama film titled Will You Love Me Tomorrow. The film revolves around a twenty-one year-old woman named Jackie (Joanne Whalley) who has spent her teenage years in institutions because she murdered three young children when she was ten. Along with a fellow inmate named Debbie (played by Tilly Vosburgh), Jackie escapes and the two women end up at the seaside with two men (played by no lesser figures than Iain Glen and Phil Daniels). Despite her terrible crimes, Jackie is a twenty-one year-old innocent who knows little about the world because she has not experienced it for herself. Will You Love Me Tomorrow was based on Mary Bell's escape from Moor Court and Joanne Whalley is for all intents and purposes playing Mary Bell in the film. This television drama film is easy to find on YouTube and certainly worth a look. Will You Love Me Tomorrow captures the sense of wonder, confusion, and terror Mary Bell must have felt when she ventured back into the world.

Mary Bell was with Stephen O'Brien for four years. After their relationship dissolved (in acrimonious fashion according to O'Brien - who didn't have anything good to say about Mary Bell later) she lived with another man. In 1988, Mary Bell was happily living in a village when her real identity was deduced by the locals. The locals (who sound really charming) demanded that Mary's four year-old daughter be removed from the local primary school. What hadn't helped Mary Bell's quest for privacy was that O'Brien had sold a story about her to one of the tabloids. The upshot of all of this was that Mary Bell and her little daughter had to pack their bags and flee - something they would soon get used to doing over the years. Mary Bell must have felt like a refugee in her own country. She later said that she was often loath to furnish a house or flat or own too many possessions because she had to be ready to move on at a moment's notice. Those who thought Mary Bell got a light sentence for her crimes were wrong. Here she was now thirty years-old but still paying a heavy price for things which happened when she was eleven. That is not a light sentence. That is a lifelong sentence. According to court documents, Mary Bell was also later identified and attacked in a pub in the early 1990s. She was often having a miserable time.

In 1993 the murder of the toddler James Bulger by two small boys shocked, outraged, and appalled Britain. Because the two killers were just ten years-old the media coverage of James Bulger's murder sometimes dredged up the case of Mary Bell as the most obvious and high profile previous example of someone this young murdering another child. One person who took a particular interest in the James Bulger murder and began to write about it was Gitta Sereny. Gitta Sereny CBE was an Austrian born author and journalist who lived in Britain from the 1950s after her American husband got a job with British Vogue. Sereny witnessed Nazi rallies in her youth and fled to France - where she had connections to the French Resistance. After the war she worked as a child welfare officer with the United Nations Relief and Rehabilitation Administration helping to return displaced children to their families and she also watched some of the Nuremberg trials (where the remaining Nazi leaders who hadn't escaped or been killed were put on trial) in person. Because of her background there were two big themes of Gitta Sereny's writing which she tended to gravitate towards - the welfare of children and the dark mystery of Nazi Germany.

In 1974, Gitta Sereny wrote a book about Franz Stangl (who was commandant of the Nazi extermination camps Sobibor and Treblinka). In the book Gitta Sereny details her meetings with Stangl and the process by which he came to acknowledge his terrible crimes. In 1995, Sereny would write a book about Albert Speer - who she knew and had talked to many times. Albert Speer (1905 – 1981) was the young architect who Hitler brought into his court. Hitler wanted Speer to rebuild Berlin into a new capital city to be known as Germania. Suffice to say, these grand plans never transpired. Speer became powerful and influential through his link to Hitler and alongside Bormann, Goebbels and Himmler was part of a quadrumvirate jostling for position and influence in the Nazi high court. By 1944 Speer (who was still only in his thirties) had been made the Armaments Minister and was responsible for the Wehrmacht having enough rifles, ammunition, tanks and vehicles to continue the war.

Speer was an advocate of "total war", the complete mobilisation of Germany's population and industry to the war effort (something which, strangely, Hitler was a late convert to, the Furhrer even demanding that confectionery factories remain open because he believed it would be bad for morale if Germans couldn't buy chocolate and sweets). But Goebbels not Speer is placed in charge of total war and uses his position to take Speer down a peg or two (both Goebbels and Martin Bormann were uncomfortable with the young Speer joining them as one of the main Nazi grandees and wasted no time in undermining him). Goebbels started taking workers out of Speer's factories to plug the manpower crisis and so Speer naturally now had a harder task in producing the weapons the army needed to fight. The petty jealousies and intrigue between the leaders of the private Nazi Empires even as the country was close to defeat continued unabated. After the war, Speer was tried at Nuremberg and sentenced to twenty years in prison. After his release, Speer became something of a celebrity, appearing on television a lot and creating an image as the "good Nazi".

The urbane Speer would claim that he knew the war was already lost when he was Armaments Minister and used his influence to save German infrastructure and industry (despite Hitler's insistence that everything in the path of the enemy should be demolished) to alleviate suffering and save the country. He said he had considered killing Hitler by putting poison gas in the Berlin bunker and knew nothing about the Holocaust. But Speer was not who he claimed to be. Not only is there evidence that he knew of the horrors of the Final Solution but he was also as responsible as anyone for the war needlessly dragging on as long as it did. Speer was remarkably ambitious and took his job as Armaments Minister very seriously, ruthlessly exploiting foreign slave labour to keep Germany's munitions factories going even as disaster and ruin loomed. Speer died of a heart attack in 1981 while in London to record a television interview.

Sereny's book about Speer exposed the truth behind his smooth façade. The fact that he must have known about the Final Solution and also the fact that he kept World War 2 going for longer than it needed to through his exploitation of slave labour. In the 1970s, Gitta Sereny became the arch nemesis of right-wing historian and Holocaust denier David Irving by forensically debunking his claims that Hitler knew nothing about the Final Solution. The first book Gitta Sereny wrote though was not about Nazi Germany at all. It was actually about Mary Bell. As someone with a keen interest in social welfare and children, Gitta Sereny became very interested in the 1968 case and trial and in 1972 published a book titled The Case of Mary Bell. Sereny was someone who looked into the soul of monsters and looked for answers so what better subject than the Demon Child of Scotswood?

Mary Bell was a morbid curiosity when Gitta Sereny wrote

the book. The media landscape back then was less magnified and more reserved than today.

Mary was not as reviled as Robert Thompson and Jon Venables (whose crimes Sereny believed were 'infinitely worse' than those of Mary Bell) in her day for what she did. BBC and ITV actually banned the Mary Bell case from news bulletins in 1968 because the case involved murdered children. This is not something which would happened today. The news channels of today would be all over the Mary Bell case. Gitta Sereny's book about Mary Bell in 1972 was more sympathetic than the general tide of feeling. Sereny looked for the humanity in Mary Bell and wondered what made her turn out that way. Gitta Sereny did not approve of Mary Bell and Norma going on trial in an adult court and found the 1968 trial (which she attended in person and followed closely) a strange and troubling spectacle. Gitta Sereny's main point in her book seemed to be her belief that rather than subject Mary Bell to a trial as if she was an adult criminal, the authorities should have been studying Mary Bell's childhood and treating her on the basis of what they found.

Gitta Sereny believed that Mary Bell had been failed by the system both in the past and the present. Sereny met and talked to all the families involved in the Mary Bell case when researching her book and evidently maintained some connections which enabled her to contact Mary Bell if she needed to. In the mid 1990s, Sereny contacted Mary Bell about her next book. Gitta Sereny wanted to write an updated companion piece to The Case of Mary Bell in which Mary Bell told her own story. Mary Bell agreed to participate and so met up with Gitta Sereny for a series of interviews. Gitta Sereny kept this all top secret and did not talk about this project in public at all. There was one particular reason above all others why this was all kept top secret. That reason was June Richardson - the dignified, highly respected, and plain speaking mother of Mary Bell's victim Martin Brown. June now campaigned for the rights of mothers who had lost children thanks to criminals. Gitta Sereny knew full well that June would be on the warpath if she knew a new book about Mary Bell featuring interviews WITH Mary Bell was coming out. Gitta Sereny therefore kept it all quiet and didn't tell the families of Martin Brown and Brian Howe.

In 1995, Mary Bell's mother Betty passed away at the age of 55. The pill popping hard drinking Betty had a tough life so it is perhaps not a huge surprise that it didn't turn out to be a long life. Betty passed away three years before the publication of a book that would blame her for just about everything and accuse her of allowing strangers to sexually abuse Mary Bell before the events of 1968. The only two people who know if this really happened are Mary and Betty but Betty was now out of the equation. Mary Bell was now the sole witness and her previous history as a witness tended to suggest she wasn't always completely reliable when it came to telling the truth. Mary Bell said her memories were confused on the sexual abuse but she believed it continued until she was about eight years-old. She claimed that the men who Betty allowed to abuse her would sometimes pick her up by the throat and throttle her until she lost consciousness because this was their kink. They liked to be rough.

Did this actually happen though or was this Mary Bell inventing a reason for why she did the same thing to children? Was this a real memory, a false memory, or Mary Bell making something up to mitigate events - much like the eleven year-old version of Mary Bell made up giving Martin Brown a quick go on a swing in a desperate attempt to explain why cotton fibres from her clothes were found on him? The one thing we can say with certainty is that Mary Bell grew up in a rough place where people had very little and prostitution, petty crime, and domestic violence was rife. There were decent respectable people in Scotswood but, sadly, Mary Bell did not grow up with decent respectable people. She grew up with a jailbird father and an alcoholic prostitute mother. Mary Bell grew up thinking that crime and domestic violence were norms rather than exceptions.

At the funeral of her mother, Mary Bell met cousins and other relatives for the first time. She said she was touched by how warmly she was greeted. However, when she met up with her sisters she found there was a distance between them which could never be navigated. She was more or less a complete stranger to them. It saddened Mary to realise that she would never have a normal relationship with her siblings. She knew that once the funeral was over they wouldn't want anything to do with her. Over the next few years Mary Bell would continue to meet with Gitta Sereny to conduct interviews for the new book. Mary Bell saw this as her chance to speak at last and lay some ghosts to rest. It had taken decades for her to even acknowledge the crimes so now she was ready for the next step. Given what happened as a result of this book, Gitta Sereny got an awful lot of criticism for putting Mary Bell back in the spotlight and thus exposing both Mary and her daughter to the risk of being unmasked.

In defence of Gitta Sereny, she was well aware of this risk and warned Mary Bell. She told Mary Bell that it was up to her if she wanted to take the risk but Mary insisted on going ahead. Gitta Sereny had hoped that the modern media was responsible enough not to turn into witch-hunters but this hope was dashed. Gitta Sereny was accused of naivety and a cold indifference the relatives of the victims but this was probably unfair. The book was well intenioned and Gitta Sereny was genuinely sorry for any distress she had caused.

What happened next was probably predictable - although the extent of the hysteria was not what Gitta Sereny had expected. The book was called Cries Unheard and drew much critical praise. When it first began to be promoted in newspapers though the families of Martin Brown and Brian Howe were spitting feathers. And then the newspapers got their teeth into the story and it all kicked off. The row went nuclear when it when it was reported that Mary Bell had been paid £50,000 (a figure Gitta Sereny disputed and said was not accurate - it was apparently £15,000) for her participation in the book.

June Richardson regarded this to be blood money. She was enraged that Mary Bell was making money off the back of her son's murder. Bookshops in Newcastle sided with June Richardson and Eileen Corrigan by refusing to stock the book. And then the politicians got involved. Tony Blair said he thought the book was distasteful and should be banned. His home secretary Jack Straw started talking about Mary Bell having no right no privacy anymore by participating in this book. It was all getting very ugly and out of control. The media and the politicians were not helping calm matters at all. Gitta Sereny said she did not tell the families of the victims about the book because she didn't know how to contact them. This was a strange excuse because Sereny was a journalist and June Richardson was surely a lot easier to contact than Mary Bell. It wouldn't take Frank Marker to track down June. Gitta Sereny, in response, to the controversy, wrote to June Richardson and Eileen Corrigan and apologised for not telling them about the book. June Richardson was not impressed with the letter and described it as patronising and an 'insult to my intelligence'.

Gitta Sereny also later appeared on breakfast television with Sharon Richardson (one of Martin Brown's sisters) and explained that the book's intent was to understand terrible deeds so that they might not happen again. She apologised to Sharon for any pain she had caused Martin's surviving relatives. Sharon Richardson was not too impressed by Cries Unheard. "I have read the book and it's not educational. All it tells you is that a if girl can kill two young children she can go on to make money and live a secret life." Brian Howe's sister Pat had a slightly different take when she was quoted in the media on the book. She had no objection to the book being published as a potentially useful academic insight into a killer's mind but she did have an objection to Mary Bell profiting financially from Cries Unheard. When it came to the money, the defence of Mary Bell was that she had always turned down this sort of thing in the past because she knew it would be seen as tasteless and morally wrong. One of her parole officers said that when she got out of prison in 1980, Mary turned down a lot of money from German publications who wanted to interview and profile her.

Mary Bell's right to privacy was now teetering on the brink of collapse. A loophole in the law had to be altered to stop newspapers in Scotland reporting Mary Bell's whereabouts and current name. It was too late to stop the payment of money to Mary Bell but Tony Blair said the government were looking at ways to stop this sort of 'thing' from happening again. It was a complex situation because most people thought the government and media should give Mary Bell a break and leave her alone. By the same token though everyone had sympathy for June Richardson and Eileen Corrigan. The last thing those two women needed was Mary Bell was back in the headlines and the money from the book was added salt into the wound. Mary Bell was now 41 years-old and her daughter was fourteen. 'We Find Mary Bell!' boomed The Sun in an article which had enough details to put Mary Bell's privacy at grave risk. The article warned that schoolchildren often walked past Mary Bell's house - as if she was going to rush out and strangle them.

The television psychiatrist Raj Persaud said that Mary Bell was a liar who wasn't telling the truth in Cries Unheard. The Sun said Mary Bell had bought a house with the money from the book. Mary Bell was now facing a lynch-mob - not from the public but the establishment and media. The Daily Mail managed to track down Stephen O'Brien, the father of Mary Bell's child. It turned out that O'Brien was in prison for burglary and drugs offences. O'Brien claimed Mary Bell left him for a man into witchcraft and said she wasn't rehabilitated. "She's not a changed woman or a reformed character. To be honest, knowing what I do about her, I can't believe she was ever allowed out, never mind going swanning round the country living on benefits." Mr O'Brien was not the most objective or reliable character witness when it came to Mary Bell so no one took his prison babblings too seriously. It sounded a lot like sour grapes because she left him for another man.

Thanks to the publication of Cries Unheard, Mary Bell was now being accused of just about everything in the newspapers. Benefits scrounging, Satanism, lies, blood money, preying on schoolchildren. This story had an unsavoury conclusion when Mary Bell and her daughter had to abandon their home and make a run for it to avoid media who had turned up. Some reporter from The Sun knocked on her door and her partner answered thinking it was the Inland Revenue. A media scrum had formed outside so Mary Bell called the police. The police arrived to protect Mary Bell and helped her and her daughter flee. Mary and her daughter were highly experienced by now when it came to having to flee at short notice. Mary Bell was living on the south coast at the time. Mary Bell's teenage daughter had no idea why her mother was so famous and had provoked this media attention so Mary had to explain it to her and tell her about what happened in 1968. Mary Bell's daughter took this revelation surprisingly well. She told her mother that she shouldn't be judged on something which happened thirty years ago when she was still a child. Mary Bell's daughter told her she was a good person and a good mother.

WHERE'S MARY?

The Daily Mirror managed to get a scoop by talking to the man Mary Bell had been living with when all this chaos engulfed her life and she had to flee. The man was only identified as 'John' and seemed to be a Geordie. He said he met Mary Bell in a Newcastle pub and they had resided in Newcastle and Northumberland before moving to the south coast. This confirmed the complaints made by Martin Brown's relatives about sightings of Mary Bell in the North East. June Richardson was annoyed about this because she always presumed Mary Bell had to stay away from Newcastle under the terms of her release. We were now getting a picture of Mary Bell's life over the last fifteen years. It was a transient life with a lot of upheaval and a reliance on benefits to make ends meet. This wasn't a life to envy very much. The only bright spot for Mary Bell was having her daughter. John said that Mary had worked in private nursing homes and also once had a job in a shop. He said there were several occasions where people worked out who Mary Bell really was but most people didn't care about that and accepted these things happened a long time ago and she wasn't that person anymore.

John said that Mary's greatest wish was to work with children but the authorities had never allowed her to do this. He blamed Mary's 'horrific' childhood for her crimes and said the social services could have prevented the events of 1968 if they'd stepped in and taken action. John said that Mary agreed to participate with Gitta Sereny's new book because she wanted to try and understand her crimes. He said Mary Bell only wanted to be forgiven and felt genuine remorse and guilt. Mary Bell, according to John, wrote poetry as a sort of therapy. Mary Bell and John had been living in a tiny flat but put a deposit down on a house thanks to money from Cries Unheard. John said the figure of £50,000 quoted in the media was not accurate. Gitta Sereny defended the payment by pointing out Mary Bell had a daughter to look after - a daughter who had nothing to do with Mary Bell's crimes and deserved the same security and safety as any child. John told the Mirror that he and Mary Bell were now skint and only had £34 in the bank. John said that Mary Bell had taken his surname and given herself a new Christian name. Mary Bell had changed her name a lot over the years.

June Richardson and Eileen Corrigan never actually met one another in the wake of the murders of 1968 which robbed them both of sons. They were finally brought together to protest against Cries Unheard and became friends. Eileen was in poor health but still fighting for Brian's memory. June Richardson had two grown up daughters and together with their mother they still marked and celebrated Martin Brown's birthday each year. June's daughters were robbed of having a brother around their own age. They couldn't help but wonder what he would be doing now were it not for Mary Bell. June said it was especially sad for her to know that she would never experience any grandchildren from Martin. The obvious question to ask now was whether Cries Unheard was worth all the fuss and upset it caused? Did it answer any questions and finally put the tin lid on the Mary Bell story? The answer to that is debatable.

1972's The Case of Mary Bell is by far the best book ever written about this case and Cries Unheard lifts an awful lot from that original book. This is probably necessary as background to the case but it does mean there often isn't much that is new if you've read the original. Gitta Sereny weaves the fresh revelations around the familiar story and also provides details on what life was like in custody for Mary Bell. The 'fresh revelations' are, as we have talked about in previous chapters, basically that Mary Bell was a victim of sexual abuse thanks to her crazy mother. This then is the explanation for why Mary Bell killed those children. She was pushed to breaking point and couldn't take any more. The violence and abuse in her home was too much. Gitta Sereny used Cries Unheard to again criticise putting Mary and Norma through a trial and also criticised the social services for not staging some sort of intervention which could have saved Martin Brown and Brian Howe.

The notion that Mary Bell was simply an evil and nasty child is dismissed by Gitta Sereny and she argues that no evil was present or intended. Gitta Sereny suggests in Cries Unheard that Britain could learn from Germany when it comes to preventing and dealing with cases like this. This suggestion is baffling given that when Cries Unheard was published Germany had four times the ratio of juvenile killers than Britain. Cries Unheard is slightly critical of Red Bank - where Mary Bell spent the most time in custody. The criticisms are not of the facilities or care because Red Bank was much better than prison. Gitta Sereny's criticisms were that Red Bank did not do enough to make Mary Bell talk about her crimes or face up to them. This was, according to Gitta Sereny, the whole point of Cries Unheard. To give Mary Bell a chance to finally address her crimes and talk about them as therapy. The other point of the book (as the title implied) was to implore the authorities to take a more proactive and interventionist role in the welfare of children. In more recent years social services have sometimes been criticised for being too interventionist so perhaps someone was listening to Gitta Sereny and her book worked and did some good.

Gitta Sereny, as she probably expected, got roses and brickbats for Cries Unheard with the roses in the clear majority. The roses praised her for a sympathetic and touching examination of the case, child abuse, and child welfare in general. The brickbats were mostly for the perception that Gitta Sereny had got too close to her subject at the risk of objectivity and displayed a strange indifference to the two victims and their surviving mothers. The family of

Martin Brown never forgave Gitta Sereny for Cries Unheard. When the author sadly died in 2012 at the age of 91, both June Richardson and her daughter Sharon told the media that, while they didn't wish death on anyone, there was a 'relief' in the family that Gitta Sereny wouldn't be able to write about Mary Bell anymore. "Mary Bell made money out of our grief," said Sharon. "This surely isn't right. The book brought it all back for us. We didn't have any say in the book, there was nothing we could do about it."

Gitta Sereny, with her laser focus on Mary Bell, never seemed very interested in June Richardson and Eileen Corrigan. There was no one to write June and Eileen's story. They had to speak for themselves. Gitta Sereny was a great woman and writer and she knew that returning to the case of Mary Bell would be controversial. This definitely proved to be the case. One thing that everyone agreed on in the wake of Cries Unheard is that Mary Bell and her daughter should be left alone. The media circus of 1998 was a vulgar spectacle. After this unwelcome taste of the spotlight, Mary Bell and her daughter managed to go to ground again. The trail went cold and the media backed off. In 2001, it was reported that Mary Bell had been used as an advisor by home office officials when it came to what should be done with the supervision of Jon Venables and Robert Thompson - the two killers of James Bulger - after their release. That same year they were granted a lifelong injunction to protect their identities. These two young people were probably the most hated people in Britain and at risk of retribution.

As for Mary Bell and her daughter, they only had a holding injunction to protect their identities and were deemed 'medium risk' by the authorities. Mary Bell, shaken by the events of 1998, wanted to change that. Under article 8 of the European convention on human rights, Mary Bell secured lifelong anonymity for herself and her daughter in May, 2003. Dame Elizabeth Butler-Sloss, president of the family division of the High Court of Justice, said that Mary Bell had lived in the 'community' for twenty-years since prison (Mary was now 46) and hadn't committed any crimes in that time. Dame Elizabeth Butler-Sloss praised Mary Bell for the job she had done raising a 'charming' daughter. The home secretary, David Blunkett, supported the lifelong anonymity because, in his words, the daughter shouldn't suffer for the crimes of the mother.

June Richardson was none too thrilled at seeing Mary Bell's name in the headlines again. June told the press she would like to see a condition of the lifelong anonymity be that Mary Bell was banned from earning any money by talking about her crimes. "The best that could happen would be for her to remain anonymous and just vanish and we can get on with our lives," June told the BBC. "They keep on talking about her privacy, but what about our privacy, our mental state, our health? After they've all finished with their cosy little court case and all the barristers have sorted her life out - who sorts my life out? It takes us months to pull our socks up and start getting on with our lives again."

What was shoddy about the Mary Bell case was how little support the relatives of the victims got. June Richardson was offered no support or counselling by the authorities. She was denied compensation to give Martin a proper headstone for his grave. She was never given any updates on what was happening to Mary Bell.

This is what irritated the families of the victims as much as anything about Cries Unheard. The fact that Gitta Sereny didn't seem to take their feelings into consideration. She seemed to have more affection and sympathy for Mary Bell. 'The murderer, whether Mary Bell or Albert Speer, is the leading character and everybody else, including the victims and their families, is relegated to a supporting role,' wrote the Observer on Cries Unheard. 'Bell is like a literary character - too interesting for a writer like Sereny to ignore. Some think that now Sereny has gone too close to the flames and that in the heat of discovering Mary Bell , lost sight of Bell's victims.' Eileen Corrigan, the mother of Brian Howe, was as sick of seeing Mary Bell headlines in the newspapers as June. "She must still be sick, if she takes that money. There's something loose somewhere. If she was cured, she would not be able to bear the money. What is the word remorse supposed to mean? And how can she accept the anonymity and the new life, and then contribute to a book and take money. That's having it both ways."

The Mary Bell story had one more headline in 2009 when the newspapers reported that Mary (who was now 51) had become a grandmother. This news did not having Martin Brown's family jumping for joy. It merely made them reflect on what they had lost and missed out on in their own family. Mary Bell had defied the odds. You wouldn't have predicted much of a future for that evil and spiteful eleven year-old girl in 1968. She ended up as a decent person and a good mother. Now she was a grandmother. The anonymity order of Mary Bell and her daughter was updated by the High Court to include the grandchild. When Ian Huntley's former girlfriend Maxine Carr was later granted anonymity it was called a 'Mary Bell order' in the press. Mary Bell's grandchild was referred to only as 'Z' in court documents. It was sometimes suggested that Mary Bell was lucky to have a daughter rather than a son. If she'd had a son, when he became four years-old, would Mary Bell have seen the faces of Martin and Brian each time she looked at him? Perhaps she did that when her daughter was four. Gitta Sereny told the press that Mary Bell was consumed by guilt and remorse. She was truly sorry for what she did in 1968.

The little May Bell of Scotswood essentially died in the early 1970s and thankfully never surfaced again. Mary Bell became a new person. Her punishment for 1968 was eleven years behind bars, media witch-hunts, and a fairly crappy life at the best of times with no money and a lot of moving around. She did though build her own family unit to mitigate the downsides. The tragedy of this case is that Mary Bell took so long to understand the importance of kindness. By the time she learned to be a human being she had condemned two mothers to a lifetime of sorrow and nightmares. Mary Bell vanished again after the grandchild news of 2009. Her identity was protected and there was nothing left to report. The story of Mary Bell had come to an end. The final scene in this film was Mary Bell playing with her grandchild. The screen has faded out on the present day Mary Bell but the 1968 version of Mary Bell is immortal. You can read about that version of Mary Bell in endless new true crime articles. That version of Mary Bell is frozen in time, trapped in that blurred photograph of the smirking little girl with the bob haircut.

Many of the current articles use the familiar questionable tropes of the Mary Bell story. She had a genius level IQ, was extraordinarily pretty, a cunning supervillain (swapping bon mots and witticisms with QC's in court), and a child prostitute who men liked to strangle. The main supporting character Norma is usually depicted as Lennie in Of Mice and Men. What if none of this was true? What if Mary Bell was just a nasty, mean and brutal little kid with no sense of right and wrong? Some crimes are impossible to explain. No one ever really explained why Mary Bell killed those two boys. Mary couldn't even explain it herself in Cries Unheard. The most logical explanation would be to say that poverty and neglect created Mary Bell. The early psychological abuse by Betty, making Mary feel unwanted by leaving her with relatives, the volatility and temper of Betty putting Mary on edge all the time. To state the obvious, Mary Bell would not have become a killer if she'd grown up in a lovely home with two middle-class doctors as her parents.

So it was poverty, lack of supervision, lack of attention, no role models at home, lack of a reliable father figure, not enough love from her mother, violence at home, and so on. You could then interpret the murders as a desperate cry for attention. But that still doesn't explain why Mary killed when millions of children have equally harsh upbringings but don't turn out bad. This makes Mary Bell not quite unique but not far off it. Mary Bell is therefore mystifying. She killed with no motive and no explanation. And this I think is one of the reasons why the families of Martin Brown and Brian Howe felt that pain, bewilderment and lack of closure their whole lives. It was because there was no explanation or reason why their loved ones died. If a person is murdered there is usually an explanation. There was an argument or a fight which escalated. They were robbed and so it was financially motivated. It was an accident. The killer was mentally disturbed and shouldn't have been on the street. The killer was sexually motivated. It was a crime of passion. It was religious fanaticism. It was terrorism. And so on.

None of these explanations were applicable to Mary Bell. So the families of Martin and Brian had no answers. They simply saw Mary Bell as pure unexplained evil and you can't really blame them. Gitta Sereny (and Mary Bell's partner 'John') apportioned a lot of the blame to Newcastle social services - which (though one can understand where they are coming from) seems unfair. You can't expect some Newcastle social worker in 1968 to report to his superiors and say, "I think we should move little May Bell of 70 Whitehouse Road to a children's home. I've had a premonition that she's about to murder two boys." June Richardson passed away on April the 21st, 2013. She was 68 years-old and had been battling cancer. There were many tributes to June from colleagues in the National Victims' Association (NVA) and Mamaa (Mothers Against Murder And Aggression). June spent her last years in a caravan in Amble, Northumberland. She was serene about the prospect of death because she believed it would finally allow her to be reunited with Martin.

The deaths of Gitta Sereny and June Richardson were like a symbolic closing of the page for the Mary Bell story. June's daughters were still around and watching closely for any signs of Mary Bell suddenly springing up in the headlines again but the controversies of 1998 were long gone now. The story was over but the story of 1968 will never be over. That story will be told endlessly. The actor and filmmaker Tony Hickson, who made a puppet short film based on Mary Bell, said that when he was a child growing up in Newcastle his grandmother would tell him scary stories about Mary Bell as if she was some mythical part of folkloric tradition. This is the fate of Mary Bell. She ended up as a horror story. The chilling thing about this horror story is that it wasn't pure fiction or folklore.

THE BAD SEED

Norma Joyce Bell did not have anonymity but she might as well have done because she became invisible not long after the trial in 1968. There are unverified reports that Norma died of cancer in 1989 at the age of 34. Norma vanishes without trace in the early 1970s and never seemed to surface again. Although she is usually depicted as stupid in the Mary Bell story there is evidence that Norma had more street smarts than Mary Bell. Norma understood that all she needed to do was tell the truth (even the horrible stuff like viewing Brian Howe's body) and Mary Bell would sink while she would float. Mary Bell was a much better talker than Norma but Norma still wiped the floor with Mary in court. It has occasionally been suggested that Norma's tearful and stuttering performance in court was a deliberate exaggeration to win sympathy. I don't think we can give this theory much credence. Norma wasn't acting. She was just being herself.

Although the young Mary is crystallised in that fuzzy black

and white picture, making her look like a childhood Clara Bow, her bold blue eyes allegedly mesmeric (and not in a good way) to all, Norma was actually better looking than Mary. It's a largely irrelevant detail but one rarely mentioned in this case. Norma had more loving and reliable parents than Mary too. Mary seemed strangely determined to drag Norma down with her in the end - or even throw Norma under the bus alone. Was there a jealous component to the way Mary was able to turn so brutally on her best friend? There are, if you look, threads in the void of cyberspace which wonder why Norma got off and argue that she was just as bad as Mary. These threads will point to the N carved in Brian Howe's stomach and then changed to an M. This is alleged to have been Norma changing the N to an M to incriminate Mary. And then the theory snowballs into Norma killing Brian and pinning the blame on Mary. Norma, 'feeble minded' Norma, is actually the criminal mastermind in this version of the tale. These speculations seem unaware though that no fibres from Norma were found on Martin Brown. They also seem unaware that Mary confessed to both murders in Cries Unheard.

The relationship between Mary and Norma is one of the most complex puzzles in this case. Neither of them ever got into trouble again when they were parted. Mary was still a bit wild in custody at first but she soon calmed down. What a fascinating meeting it would have been if Mary and Norma had met up again when they were adults and mothers. That meeting couldn't happen and neither (one presumes) would have welcomed it but the bond they shared was powerful and ultimately destructive. When they were in court, Mary and Norma blamed one another in their evidence and would shake their head or sigh when the other was saying something they didn't like or agree with. Sometimes though they would make eye contact and stare at one another in acknowledgment, almost a sort of understanding. You get the impression, and it may be a mistaken impression, that if Mary and Norma had been banged up together they would have instantly become firm friends again.

The conspiracy theories in this case still abound - though in relative obscurity. There is, for example, a theory that Mary Bell played Gitta Sereny in the same way that Myra Hindley played Lord Longford. This theory would contend that Mary Bell played the authorities too in custody - merely pretending to be cured. There is an obvious problem with this specific conspiracy theory. Mary Bell WAS cured. Since her release in 1980 she hasn't harmed a fly. It is possible for those who committed awful crimes to reform and live a productive and peaceful life. Jasmine Richardson (who we talked about in a previous chapter) seems to have done this. Karla Homolka is a Canadian serial killer who, along with her then-husband Paul Bernardo, was involved in the sexual assaults and murders of at least three young women in the early 1990s, including her sister Tammy. The crimes were particularly heinous, involving brutal violence. Homolka struck a plea deal with prosecutors, agreeing to testify against Bernardo in exchange for a reduced sentence. She served twelve years in prison and was released in 2005. Her case, along with the details of the crimes, sparked public outrage and led to significant media attention.

After serving her sentence, Homolka has largely tried to live a private life; however, she has remained a controversial figure. This is the bottom line for Mary Bell, Jasmine Richardson, and Karla Homolka. Their crimes will follow them to the grave - no matter how normal or decent their later lives were. When she dies, the obituaries for Mary Bell will not talk about how nice she was to her grand-daughter or how she was really kind to her elderly neighbour. They will not talk about her poetry or how funny she was. The obituaries will use up most of their ink talking about how she murdered two boys. James Gordon Wolcott murdered his entire family in 1967 when he was fifteen years-old. Wolcott later became a professor of psychology at Millikin University in Decatur, Illinois. It is possible for even the worst people to turn their lives around. Jon Venables is back in prison today because of his child porn offences. However, Robert Thompson, who was equally responsible for James Bulger's murder, is apparently doing ok and hasn't got into trouble again. Thompson was said to be a good academic student while incarcerated and turned out to be surprisingly intelligent.

There is a very good and sound reason why we don't put ten year-olds in charge of anything. Their brains haven't developed. They still have a long way to go before they become fully formed. Once her brain developed and she grew up, Mary Bell was doubtless as perplexed as anyone by the crimes her ten and eleven year-olf self committed. This is why it was controversial to some that Mary was tried in an adult court. Mary Bell implied in Cries Unheard that she didn't really understand what she was doing and had no idea that Martin Brown and Brian Howe might be erased forever by her actions. Her conduct in the wake of the murders implied that she did have an understanding of what she had done. How much of an understanding is open to debate. This was one of the flaws in Mary Bell's later testimony. If she didn't understand death why was she asking to look in Martin Brown's coffin? Why was she keeping a log of dead relatives in her copy of the Bible?

In the enjoyably melodramatic and sinister 1956 film The Bad Seed (which was based on a play and a novel of the same name), Patty McCormack plays eight-year old Rhoda Penmark. Rhoda is precocious and sweet on the surface but in reality she's a cold hearted psycho. She murders a boy named Claude Daigle because he had the temerity to beat her in a school penmanship competition. Claude's death is mistaken for drowning (when it fact it was Rhoda who attacked him and then stopped him getting out of the river) and Rhoda's mother is worried she might be affected by the death of a schoolmate. Rhoda isn't affected at all though. She genuinely doesn't care that a boy lost his life - and all because of her too. Rhoda is willing to do anything required to cover her tracks and it slowly but surely dawns on the mother that her cute pigtailed daughter is a raving sociopath. Rhoda Penmark was a name that got bandied around a lot in 1968 when Mary Bell was convicted. This is the fictional character she was compared to the most. Still is in fact.

The Mary Bell case seems weirdly connected by articles today to the peadophobic sub-genre of horror which has given us everything from The Omen to Children of the Corn. The classic science fiction film Village of the Damned (based on the 1957 novel The Midwich Cuckoos by John Wyndham) concerns the sleepy village of Midwich, where the entire population mysteriously falls unconscious for 24 hours. When they wake up, it transpires that every woman of child-bearing age is now pregnant. The children born from these pregnancies possess powerful telepathic abilities and display cold, emotionless behaviour. The film delves into the ethical dilemmas involved in dealing with extraordinary and possibly malevolent children. By blurring Mary Bell into this world of fiction we almost give her too much credit. Mary Bell was really not that calculating or extraordinary. She was fairly easy to catch and gave herself away in a number of ways. She was no threat to adults - only children (the one area where Mary Bell displayed shrewdness - and cowardice too - was in selecting victims who were much smaller and no physical threat).

The chilling thing about Mary Bell's crimes is that they were done by what seemed to be an ordinary and average child and took place in the real world. The social services and police in Scotswood probably had Mary Bell low odds for a future of petty crime and thievery but no one could have guessed she would kill other children. For some reason, there seems to be more of a public outcry when children kill. It goes against nature and all of our assumptions. Children are supposed to be innocent and gentle. Most of them are but history is dotted with bad seeds like Mary Bell. There were killer children long before Mary Bell but many of these cases were lost to time or never reported. These days we seem to have feral kids who carry knives and machetes around with them. This is mostly gang related and so doesn't have much in common with the likes of Mary Bell and the Bulger killers but when we see stories of these grim feral zombie kids with knives we immediately find ourselves wondering who the parents of these kids are and why they've done such a terrible parenting job.

That was the crux of Gitta Sereny's thesis on Mary Bell over two books. Who were Mary Bell's parents? What was going on inside 70 Whitehouse Road? Gitta Sereny felt the social services and authorities should have spent a lot more time asking this question both during and before 1968. She thought Red Bank should have been asking that question too.

At the time of writing Mary Bell is 67 years-old. She lives a private life under an assumed name, pottering about in welcome obscurity. Perhaps she bakes cakes and has her daughter and grand-daughter over for Christmas. Maybe she likes gardening. Mary Bell has complete control over this version of Mary Bell. However, there is another Mary Bell who has a very public profile and is still endlessly discussed and profiled. This is the Mary Bell of 1968. That version of Mary Bell, the Bad Seed, has taken on a life of her own and is trapped forever as the villain in a black and white horror film.

The current Mary Bell would dearly wish for the other Mary Bell to cease from existing. She'd love it if the other Mary Bell had never become famous at all. Sadly for this placid 67 year-old grandmother, the horrible legend of the other Mary Bell lives on. There are punk bands named after her. You can find Mary Bell fanart online - piercing cold blue eyes firmly fixed on you with sinister intent. People who have never heard of Mary Bell will forever discover the story of this notorious little girl on crime forums and Reddit threads and be shocked by what they read. No one is sadder about all of this than Mary Bell. If she could go back in time and alter the events of 1968 she would. But she can't and so for the rest of her life has to live with what she did. That is a sentence you wouldn't wish on anyone. Not even Mary Bell.

SOURCES

https://www.thenorthernecho.co.uk
https://www.newspapers.com
https://www.bbc.co.uk
https://www.theguardian.com
https://www.thefreelibrary.com
https://en.wikipedia.org
https://www.youtube.com

PHOTO CREDIT

https://www.pexels.com/photo/close-up-on-woman-blue-eye-lit-up-by-sun-11417680/

Bruno Abdiel

Feb 28, 2022